I0083074

THOMAS S. HARRINGTON

THE
TREASON
OF THE
EXPERTS

Covid and the Credentialed Class

BROWNSTONE INSTITUTE

Copyright © 2023 Brownstone Institute (Austin, Texas),
Creative Commons Attribution International 4.0.

Physical ISBN: 9781630695880
Digital ISBN: 9781630695873

Cover art: Vanessa Mendozzi

THOMAS S. HARRINGTON

THE TREASON OF THE EXPERTS

Covid and the Credentialed Class

BROWNSTONE INSTITUTE

CONTENTS

FOREWORD TO TREASON OF THE EXPERTS

Professor Thomas Harrington's primary field of study is Hispanic culture and history, with a focus on Catalonian language, history and nationalism. One might suppose that such a person might not necessarily possess the perspicacity to see the treason of an entire class of experts from government, technology, business, medicine, and media. And yet he did: and from the very beginning of the Covid crisis. This book collects only part of his tremendously insightful observations from the beginning until recently.

Because I've come to know Tom as a friend, I have my own theory about what gave him such insight. With a deep knowledge of the life of a particular region and language group, he cultivated a keen insight into the difference between what is authentic and organic to a social order and what is exogenous and imposed by a ruling-class structure. He has a particular curiosity about the latter. His profound awareness of this power in operation in world events allowed him to see what so many others missed: namely he knew something was very off from the beginning.

He and I come from very different traditions of thought and yet we both came to the same conclusions at the same time though from different angles. My formation in economics trained me to marvel in the spontaneous orders of unplanned human interaction. His outlook trained him to sniff out and see the opposite: that which we take for granted which does not result from unplanned order but which is instead imposed and shaped by complex and interactively powerful forces that gain advantage from their invisibility. The combination of these two perspectives has made for a strong intellectual and personal bond, though I have to admit that his outlook has proven more fruitful for understanding the Covid crisis.

It's to the eternal disgrace of so many elites in the political, economic, cultural, and academic world that so many participated in the "great reset" and, further, that so many who did not participate remained silent even as essential social, market, and cultural functioning was systematically dismantled by force with the full participation of the commanding heights of society. It mortifies me as a libertarian that big business was such a willing executioner. Tom, as a decidedly left-leaning intellectual, was equally mortified to see the participation by academia and government in such destructive actions that were clearly designed to transfer wealth and power away from the social firmament to ruling-class overlords. It was a war of the ruling class against the people, and in nearly every country in the world, all in the guise of pathogenic control.

Being on the editorial end of Brownstone Institute's operations, I can report my excitement when an essay by Tom arrives in my inbox. I know for certain that I will learn something new, be encouraged to turn the prism in a different direction and observe events and trends from a new perspective, and feel infused by the power of his mind and erudition that emanates from his spectacular writing talent. In so many ways, each essay is a gift. A full book of them is a windfall, and just what we need to understand what has happened to us and where to go from here.

I'm very proud to call Tom a colleague and thrilled that he chose Brownstone as his publisher. Prepare yourself for a real adventure, one that seems often more like fiction than reality. It is inconceivable that a book like this could have appeared only a few years ago. No one would have believed it if it had. But these are extraordinary times and they require extraordinary and brave minds to operate as tour guides, as with Dante and Virgil. The treason of experts has indeed landed us in very dark places but we can see our way out with the truths elucidated herein.

Jeffrey Tucker

President, Brownstone Institute
February 5, 2023

INTRODUCTION

Like many people, I am often asked how many children were in my family growing up, and where I was in the mix. When I reply that "I grew up in the middle of five," I often receive good-natured ribbing about how I must have been—take your pick—the most difficult, confused or impractical of my parents' children. To which I always reply, "No. Actually, I was most fortunate of the group because my marginally forgotten status allowed me to observe the functioning of our family unit from a place of relative distance and calm, an experience that I like to think has served me quite nicely in life."

If having more autonomy and reflective space was the best part of being in the middle of the gang, then not having a fixed "tribe within the tribe" was probably the least. To be in the center of a closely packed group was to be neither one of the "big kids" nor one of the "little kids" but rather someone who, in the more mass-production forms of child-rearing prominent in the 1960s, might find himself placed in one camp or the other on parental whim.

Though we don't like to think of them this way, families are, among many other positive things, also systems of power. And like most systems of power, they rely, as the Italian writer Natalia Ginzburg reminds us in her marvelous autobiographical novel *Lessico Famigliare* (*Family Sayings*), heavily on the deployment of language and recurrent rhetorical patterns, verbal customs that for obvious reasons, overwhelmingly flow downward from the parents to the children.

It was, I think, owing to a desire to palliate the sometime sense of being at the mercy of parental caprice, as well as the need to fit in on a moment's notice with different familial subcultures and their distinct lexicons, that I early on became highly attuned to the reality and power of verbal codes, a curiosity that I have been fortunate to parlay into a lifelong vocation.

What does it take, as in my case, to enter into a number of other national cultural systems as an adult and gain something closely approximating a native understanding of their internal dynamics?

First of all, it involves a gift for rapid pattern recognition, of sounds, of grammatical structures, and of common lexical and phonetic transformations. But arguably more important in the long run is a capacity to quickly locate and assimilate the historical, ideological, and aesthetic cliches that organize the life of the cultural collective you are seeking to understand; that is, the set of stories that same collective tells itself to make sense of the world.

Once you immerse yourself in this process of story-gathering, another question inevitably arises. Where do these enveloping social narratives come from?

During much of the latter part of the 20th century, the most common answer to this query among academics was they trickle up from the "spirit of the ordinary people." In time, however, this explanation—which not coincidentally nicely ratified the notions of participatory democracy being promoted by Western governments in the wake of World War II—lost sway, with students of identity-making returning in more recent years to an answer that had previously been seen as self-evident: mostly from the lettered elites.

It was and is these cultural entrepreneurs—scholars began to once again to admit—who, often backed by very large pecuniary interests, have always had a grossly outsized role in determining what the great mass of a given population comes to see as social "reality."

Particularly instrumental in helping me see the creation of social "realities" in this way was the work of the cultural theorist Itamar Even-Zohar. The Israeli scholar not only provides us with abundant proof of the outsized role of elites in the making of culture throughout history, but convincingly asserts that, with enough archival digging, it is possible to effectively "map" the trajectory of a given set of social tropes from its invention and promotion by an individual or small group of thinkers, to its effective consecration as an unquestionable social "truth."

To begin thinking and acting in these terms is, as I have suggested elsewhere, "to embark on a program of observational detoxification." You begin to let the reports produced in the "prestige" media and much of academia, which you once imbued with considerable credibility, drift by your ears and eyes with little notice, and instead turn your attentions toward finding out all you can about the institutions and other clusters of power that have generated the rhetorical frames and ideological presumptions that effectively govern the parameters of what mainstream journalists and academics are allowed to think and say.

In time, clear patterns emerge, to the point where you can begin to predict the general upshot of the messages that will soon emanate from the mouths of public figure "X" or public figure "Y" in most circumstances. Similarly, if you listen and read closely across supposedly distinct media platforms you can begin to observe clear evidence of messaging replication rooted in the fact that the ostensibly antithetical information outlets depend, in the end, on the same rhetorical frames supplied by the same structures of power.

Doing this type of detective work today is, strangely, easier than at any time in the past.

One reason is the existence of the internet.

Another, arguably more important factor is the increasing brazenness of our sign-making elites; a product, it seems, of their ever-increasing power and, with it, ever more open disdain for the intelligence of the citizenry.

We've all seen parents who, when seeking to lead and persuade their children, talk to them in respectful tones, and those who, in contrast, resort quickly to screaming and insults to achieve their controlling ends.

Since its entry into World War I, if not before, the US has had a highly sophisticated domestic propaganda system designed to support its mission as an imperial power and bulwark of the global capitalist system. And for much of that time, those in the media and in academia who were aligned with its aims generally spoke to us like the "calm parent" mentioned above.

In the wake of September 11th, however, things changed. Subtlety was tossed out the window, and we were all forced into the role of the children of those ugly, screaming parents.

As horrible as it was, the propagandists' lack of subtlety afforded those of us who were able to keep our minds in the face of this informational brutality with an extraordinary opportunity to increase our understanding of the nexus between state-corporate Big Power and Big Media.

During the first decade of the century, for example, the Neocons basically dared us to draw maps of the interlocking directorships through which they had effectively gained control of the US foreign policy establishment and its accompanying media apparatus. And they gave the careful observer more than enough material for the publication of several handbooks on how not to get duped again by their fear-driven, "problem-reaction-solution" approach to fomenting mass political mobilization and abrupt, top-down cultural change.

So blatant and unsubtle were the methods of bamboozlement used, and so horrible was the bloodletting and cultural destruction they made possible at home and abroad, that I, and I suspect many others were quite sure that we would never let a similar propaganda entrapment happen to us again.

And then came that fateful day in March 2020 when, using all the same informational terror techniques, with even less subtlety than before if that is possible, the state and its attendant media apparatus did it to us again. And a majority of the country, it seems, responded not like self-possessed adults capable of learning from past mistakes, but rather frightened and long-abused children. Maybe the screaming campaign after September 11th had affected the inner psyches of our fellow countrymen more profoundly than many of us were prepared to believe.

The Treason of the Experts[1]

While the propaganda blitz after September 11th was impressive in its force and scope, those directing it were from a small fairly readily identifiable cadre of intellectual agitators, housed in well-known think-tanks,

---

1 If the title of the book sounds vaguely familiar to you, it is meant to. *The Treason of the Intellectuals* is a celebrated 1927 book in which the French intellectual Julien Benda denounced how, during World War I (for me, the best historical correlate we have to the enveloping madness of the Covid era) both French and German intellectual abandoned their appointed role as truth-seekers and became recyclers and enforcers of rabid government propaganda.

in transparently ideological publications and in key, captured nodes of the corporate media. True, there was also a degree of spontaneous support for the aggressive American response to the attacks in a few other sectors of America's college-educated cohort. But in general, the "expert" class, by which I mean those in the liberal professions possessing post-graduate degrees, were generally cautious when not outright hostile to the Bush administration's wars of choice. And in this sense, they remained true to the function they had assumed as a group in the wake of the protests against the Vietnam war.

But this time around, these privileged people, whose educational background putatively provided them with greater critical thinking skills than most, and hence an enhanced ability to see through the barrage of propaganda, fell immediately and massively into line.

Indeed, not only did we see them overwhelmingly accept the government's repressive, unproven and often patently unscientific measures to contain the Covid virus, but watched many of them emerge online and in other public forums as semi-official enforcers of repressive Government policies and Big Pharma marketing pitches.

We watched as they mocked and ignored world-class doctors and scientists, and for that matter, anyone else who expressed ideas that were at variance with official government policies. They told us, ridiculously, that science was not a continuous process of trial and error, but a fixed canon of immutable laws, while promoting, on that same absurd basis, the establishment and enforcement of medical apartheid within families and communities.

We saw how, in the name of keeping their children safe from a virus that could do them virtually no harm, they greatly impeded their long-term social, physical and intellectual development through useless mask-wearing, social distancing and screen-based learning.

And in the name of protecting the elderly, they promulgated medically useless rules that forced many older people to suffer and die alone, deprived of the comfort of their loved ones.

And they topped all this off by rabidly backing the idea that every citizen of the Republic, including those same functionally immune children, be injected—under the patently illegal and immoral threat of losing their job and their fundamental rights to bodily autonomy and freedom of movement—with an experimental drug that was known to be incapable of doing the first thing a vaccine should be able to do: stop the transmission of the supposedly ultra-mortal virus.

But perhaps most frightening and striking of all was, and still is, the way so many of these people, who by dint of their educational backgrounds should have found it more easy than most to go to the primary sources of scientific information on the virus and the measures taken to lessen its impact, chose in large numbers—with doctors being very prominent among them—to instead "educate" themselves on these important matters with curt summaries derived from the mainstream press, social media or Pharma-captured agencies like the CDC and the FDA. This, paradoxically, while millions of intrepid and less credentialed people with a greater desire to know the truth, often became quite knowledgeable about the actual state of 'the science."

This devastating case of class abdication—which essentially turned the old adage about "To whom much is given, much is expected" on its head—is a central focus of this book.

Viewed more broadly, this is one man's chronicle, at times indignant and at others reflective, of an extraordinary moment in the history of the world, a moment of crisis whose eventual resolution will have far-reaching consequences for our children and their children.

Will we renew our trust in the dignity, moral autonomy and inherent miraculousness of each individual human being? Or will we, in our absent-minded drift away from the only true sources of life and spiritual renewal—things like love, friendship, wonder and beauty—resign ourselves to the idea of living a new version of medieval serfdom, wherein our bodies and our minds are seen as, and used by, our self-appointed masters as a renewable resource for the execution of their megalomaniacal dreams?

This is the choice before us. I know which reality I prefer. What about you?

CHENEY'S "ONE PERCENT DOCTRINE" COMES TO THE FIELD OF PUBLIC HEALTH

will begin with the necessary preventions. I am not an epidemiologist nor do I have any medical expertise. I have, however, spent a great deal of time over the years looking at how deployment of information affects the making of public policy. It is in this vein that I articulate the speculations that follow. I hold no claims to being absolutely correct, or even substantially so. Rather, I am simply seeking to raise some issues that may have been overlooked thus far in the government/media rendering of the Corona crisis.

Three days ago, *El País* in Madrid, which likes to think of itself as the *New York Times* of the Spanish-speaking world, ran an article with the following headline: "Young, Healthy and in the ICU: the Risk is There." The journalist then went on to tell the story of how an apparently healthy 37-year-old Spanish policeman had died the day before. After this, he shared statistics from the prestigious British medical journal *The Lancet* on the patterns of mortality related to the Coronavirus in Italy, saying:

> ...the median age of the deceased is 81 and more than two thirds of these people had diabetes, cardiovascular diseases or were ex-smokers. 14 percent were over 90 years of age, 42 percent were between 80 and 89, 32.4 percent between 70 and 79, 8.4 percent between 60 and 69, and 2.8 percent between 50 and 59. In that country on the other side of the Alps (Italy) the deaths of people under 50 are anecdotal and there are no known deaths of anyone under 30.

Later, he adduced a chart from the Italian Institute of Heath showing the chances of death from Covid-19 in each of the ten-year age blocks from 0 to 100. Here they are:

0-9 years, 0 percent
10-19 years, 0 percent
20-29 years, 0 percent;
30-39 years, 0.1 percent
40-49 years, 0.1 percent
50-59 years 0.6 percent
60-69 years, 2.7 percent
70-79 years, 9.6 percent
80-89 years, 16.65 percent
90+ years, 19 percent
Data lacking on 3.2 percent of cases.

Assuming that the information cited is correct, we can arrive at some provisional conclusions.

The first and most immediate one is that the writer at *El País* or the editors that came up with the title for the article are guilty of serious journalistic malpractice. The headline, combined with the anecdote about the 37-year-old fallen policeman, clearly suggests to readers that young and healthy people need to be aware that they too are in significant danger of dying from the Coronavirus. However, the statistics from Italy in no way support this notion.

The second one is that infection *per se* does not seem to present a serious health risk to the overwhelming majority of people under 60. This, of course, presumes that rates of infection in the 0-60 age cohort are as least as high as in the older group, something that makes a lot of sense when we consider the obviously greater mobility of these people relative to their co-citizens with ages between 60-100.

The third conclusion, which follows from the previous two, would seem to be that the best way to attack the problem is to concentrate the overwhelming focus of social efforts on isolating and treating people in the 60 to 100 age bloc, while also allocating places for those relatively few under 60 who become seriously symptomatic.

What these statistics do not tell us much about, nor am I in any way expert or informed enough about to include in my calculus, is just how many hospital places are required to keep the under 60 mortality statistics as low as they currently are. If the number of hospital places required to treat these people is extremely high, then this could cancel out much of what I have said up until now.

If anyone has any statistics on this, I would appreciate seeing them. Assuming, however, that the use of hospital spaces by under 60s is not excessively heavy, it seems licit to ask why the effort to attack the virus seems directed at curbing its spread in the population as a whole rather than on treating those clearly most at risk of dying from the disease.

Or to put it another way, does it really make sense to bring an entire society to a crashing halt, with the enormous and unforeseen long-term economic and social consequences that this will have, when we know that most of the working population could, it seems, continue to go about their business without any real risk of mortality? Yes, some of these younger people would suffer through some very nasty days in bed, or even spend some time in the hospital, but at least the societal breakdown we are currently experiencing would be avoided.

In 2006, the journalist Ron Suskind wrote a book called the *The One Percent Doctrine* in which he examined Dick Cheney's outlook on what he and many others like to call the problem of anti-US "terror." The "one percent doctrine" holds, in short, that if someone high up in the power structure in Washington believes that there is a one-percent chance of some foreign actor wanting to seriously harm the United States' interests or citizens anywhere in the world, then he or she has the right, if not the duty to eliminate (read: "kill") that potential actor, or set of potential actors, immediately.

I think that anyone who believes in minimal notions of reciprocity and fair play among individuals and groups can perceive the madness in this posture which essentially says the slightest notion of insecurity *as subjectively perceived by the US intelligence community* is enough to warrant the destruction of small and large groups of "other people."

In a country putatively spawned by the Enlightenment, and hence a belief in thorough rational analyses of problems, this turns the lightest of suspicions into a warrant for enacting the most grave type of action a government can take. In so doing, it throws the idea of doing what supposedly pragmatic Americans are best at—rigorous cost-benefit analyses—completely out the window.

And nearly two decades after the adoption of this posture, the death, destruction, financial depletion and overall rise in tensions between the countries of the world generated by this policy prescription are there for all to see.

So if, as suggested, the narcissistic madness of this is plain to see for anyone who takes the time to calmly mentally game the effects of such a policy over the long haul, how is it that we have essentially come to—mostly silently—accept it as normal?

Because the people in power, aided by a compliant media, have gotten very good at plying us with largely decontextualized but emotionally evocative visual images. Why? Because they know, based on studies by their own experts in "perception management," that such things have a way of dramatically arresting the analytical capabilities of even the most apparently rational people.

Another technique used is that of reducing problems, even the most complicated ones rooted deeply in history and possessing potentially far-reaching and broad social consequences, down to simple personal story lines. In this way we are further encouraged to blunt any inclination we might have to delve into the complexities of these issues, or the long-term steps we might take to remedy them.

All of which brings us back to the problem of the Coronavirus and the way it is being portrayed in the media, and from there, handled in public policy.

Why, for example, are we constantly being told about the gross numbers of infections? If the Italian statistics are in any way predictive of what we should expect here, why should that be such an obsessive focus of concern?

The same might be said about all the reports about all the young and middle-aged athletes and celebrities who have tested positive for the virus. If we have a very good idea that these people will face no truly serious consequences as a result of the infection, why are we focusing so much on them, and effectively leveraging the supposed danger they find themselves in, as a reason to propagate draconian society-wide policies, with all that such policies imply in terms of spreading out already scarce resources that could be better used to serve the people we know to be facing the greatest danger from this apparent plague?

To be infected with AIDS in the early years of that plague was—at least we were told—to receive a near certain death sentence. This is far from the case when it comes to the Coronavirus. And yet we are treating "testing positive" for it with the same, if not more solemnity, than we ever did in the case of AIDS.

As I write, I can hear some readers muttering "How would this SOB feel if his son or daughter were one of the few young people to be killed by the virus?" I would, of course, be devastated in a way that I cannot even begin to fathom.

But the fear that something bad might happen to me, my family or a relatively small group of people—and yes, according to the Italian example, we are talking about a relatively small number of people under fifty who are in any mortal danger—is no way to make policy for national communities.

Sound harsh?

It shouldn't. With the aid of actuaries, governments and large industries are constantly and quite coldly calculating how much loss or shortening of human life they must concede as inevitable in order to achieve putatively larger and more socially enveloping goals. At the Pentagon, for example, you can be sure people regularly compute how many young soldier lives can and should be sacrificed to achieve goal X or goal Y in support of our supposed national interests.

Curious isn't it that at a time when our leaders are assiduously employing martial language to garner citizen support in the "war" against the Coronavirus, the rational considerations on the disposability of life they regularly employ and accept as normal are suddenly suspended.

A case of hysteria getting the best of them? Or could it be that they, following Rahm Emanuel's famously cynical advice, might have decided not to let a serious crisis go to waste?

We can and should debate the true magnitude of what we are going through and whether it merits the radical suspension of our economic and social order.

From where I sit, the best course would seem to be that of focusing energies like a laser on those most likely to suffer and die, while leaving those who, according to the Italian statistics, appear to be largely free of this danger to continue to row the ship of state in this terrible time of devastation and worry.

22 March 2020

NEW CORONA CASES: THE ULTIMATE FLOATING SIGNIFIER

I f there is one thing that Saussure's revolution in linguistic thinking taught us it is that all semantic meaning is relational; that is, that words or terms seldom have a fixed meaning. Rather, they gather their meaning in any given moment through their relationship with the other words or terms with which they are deployed. Even-Zohar, among others, has taken these insights into the broader field of culture and taught us to observe the perpetual dynamics of symbolic repertoires in a similar way.

For example, while most of us today presume, given our cultural training, that Shakespeare is a transcendent genius who will always be recognized as such, we have to be open to the idea that at some point in the future, the contextual armature that makes this appear self-evident to us might not be there for others, and that they may, in fact, cast him aside in their canonizing efforts for, say, Erica Jong or Howard Fast.

The key term here is "contextual armature"; that is, the set of relations, implied or explicit, that give a word or term its meaning in any given moment.

When we speak of floating or empty signifiers we are referring to words or terms whose contextual armature is so vague or unclear as to deprive us of the ability to derive any stable sense of meaning from them.

In recent decades, political leaders and the press that increasingly works to pimp the population on their behalf have come to see the enormous value that semantically empty, if at the same time, emotionally evocative signifiers can have in mobilizing the populations they lead to act in one form or another.

"Weapons of Mass Destruction" is a classic example in this regard. What is particularly meant here is vague. But that's just it. They really don't want us to have a conversation aimed at actually regressing the chain (or lack thereof) of relations undergirding the term. They imply that it is something really bad and leave it at that, so as to incite a vague sense of dread inside our brains. And all too many of us are content to leave it there without further relational exploration

Today we are inundated with daily reports about new "corona cases" which are clearly meant to be seen as a bad thing in and of themselves. But do we really have the relational information needed to jump to that conclusion?

First of all there is the question of testing, and the fact that the number of infected people might be much larger than we know and that the vast majority of them may have already had and overcome the disease and are effectively immune to it. There is also the apparent fact that the vast majority of "cases" do not require hospitalization nor do they, according to Italian and Spanish statistics, result in death. Indeed, if one believes in the idea of herd immunity, which has been the way the human organism in its collectivity has defeated viruses again and again over history, the rise in "cases" could be seen as a good thing. In short, the term "new corona cases" may in fact mean a lot less than our media regularly suggests to us that it does.

The same could be said about the term "corona deaths." The ability to tease out the exact cause of death in people with multiple pathologies is notoriously difficult and the methods for assigning a definitive viral cause in such matters differ greatly from place to place.

It would seem that the only non-floating signifier we have at this point for judging the magnitude of what we are up against as a mortal threat is to measure the number of excess deaths (the number this year as opposed to those recent non-corona years) in places where the virus has hit hard.'

Strange, isn't it, how this more relationally solid measure is almost wholly lacking in our conversations at a time when largely empty, and highly emotionally evocative signifiers like "new corona cases" inundate our news and our consciousness?

3 April 2020

TECHNOCRATS AND AUTHORITARIANISM

I t is important in these days of constant calls to heed the advice of "experts" on the spread of the Coronavirus to recall the intimate historical links between the concept of technocracy and the practice of authoritarianism.

As soon as the ideal of a truly representative democracy moved to the center of European and American life at the end of the 19th century, those slated to lose power under this new social order began touting the advent of a supreme modern wisdom, transcendent of disputes, that would spare us all the inherent messiness and inefficiency of government by and for the people.

Interestingly, Spain played a key role in the development of this ideological current.

During the 1920s and 1930s it took on a form known as "anti-parliamentarianism," which held that only a clairvoyant class of military patriots, unencumbered by ideology, could save the country from the immobilism and corruption generated by party politics.

When, after the Spanish Civil War and World War II, the idea of social salvation by men in uniform had lost much of its earlier luster, these efforts to save the people from themselves became increasingly focused on men of science, broadly understood. The term technocrat first came into wide usage in the late 1950s when Spanish dictator Francisco Franco entrusted the management of his country's economy to a group of thinkers from the ultra-right wing Catholic organization *Opus Dei*.

These men, who would engineer a shift from a policy of nativist protectionism to one much more centered on foreign investment were many things. But people without ideology, they were not. That, however, did not prevent the regime, and its many new banker friends around the world from presenting them as exactly this. And sadly many outside observers came to believe it.

The central conceit of technocratic thought was, and is, that there exists in data-based, scientific knowledge a clarity, that if bottled and distributed correctly, will free us from all types of noisome and unproductive debate.

However, both the past and present proponents of this wonderfully appealing construct tend to forget a very important thing: that those who collect data and interpret it are social beings, who are therefore also political beings, and thus, by definition, non-objective in their selection and deployment of the "facts."

This makes their pose of being above politics perniciously dangerous for society. Why? Because it puts all of us in the position of having to implicitly accept their wisdom as neutral, and beyond retort, even as they actively inscribe it with all sorts of epistemological and ideological biases.

There is perhaps no more clear example of this than recent campaigns to free the internet from so-called "fake news" and supposed efforts to "incite violence."

In regard to the first goal mentioned here, it should be remembered that truth, especially truth in socially-nested acts and political positions only ever exists in approximate form.

Or to put it more simply, outside the world of basic affirmations of very concrete material realities, there is no such thing as 100 percent real news. Rather, there is a spectrum of interpretive possibilities regarding the verisimilitude of the claims being made by various actors about this or that phenomenon. Seriously getting to the bottom of things is always a relatively disordered and uncertain business that seldom results in unassailable conclusions.

And yet we now have companies tied umbilically to the US-EU-Israeli axis of military and business power now telling us that they have algorithms that can free us from that inherent messiness by eliminating "fake news" from our screens.

Do you really think they have no ulterior motive in offering this supposed service to us? Do you really think that the operative notions of "fakeness" and "misinformation" in their algorithms won't in some way, perhaps even in large measure, be conflated with ideas those from this power configuration view as having the potential to undermine their particular strategic goals?

In regard to the aim of freeing us from hate speech and incitement to violence, is it really objectively true – indeed can it ever be determined to be objectively true – that singing the praises on the Internet of, say Hezbollah, is inherently more an incitement to violence than praising the US military and its mortal powers in the ways that have become almost obligatory in our public spaces and celebrations?

Though you or I might not see it that way, the paramilitary group based in southern Lebanon is, for many around the world, a heroic resistance force that is fighting against what they see as serial encroachments upon their land and their way of life.

And then there is the not so small matter of numbers of people maimed and killed. When we look at the statistics side-by-side there is not even a shadow of a doubt as to who has killed or maimed more people in the Middle East. The US military is so absurdly ahead in this game of – to use one well-known definition of terrorism – employing "violence or the threat of violence, especially against civilians, in the pursuit of political goals," it isn't even funny.

But the last I heard, no algorithm was being developed for saving the denizens of cyberspace from those fulsomely praising our championship killing machine. This, even when its online partisans use hyper-aggressive and ethnically insulting language to justify past murders, or to bless the commission of new ones.

And yet, this grossly disparate treatment of two fighting forces, which can only be explained in terms of the embedded ideological predilections of those running the operation, is consistently presented to us in the language of above-the-fray technical neutrality.

That most people in the country apparently buy into this transparently lame technocratic apology for flat-out discourse control is perhaps the most frightening aspect of it all.

If we are really interested in democracy, we cannot passively cede to the ethos of technocratic management that our lazy and cowardly politicians and their media servants are now relentlessly foisting upon us.

15 April 2020

WHEN CONSUMERISM LOCKS DEATH AND DIMINISHMENT AWAY IN THE BACK ROOM

Most of us, I suspect, have had the experience of walking into a darkened room we presume to be empty, only to find someone sitting silently in the shadows observing our movements. When this happens, it is, initially at least, an unnerving experience. Why? Because, though we don't often speak about this, there are things we do, think about, and say to ourselves when alone that we would never allow ourselves to do, think about, or say to ourselves in the presence of others.

When seeking to understand what Bourdieu called the "structuring structures" of a culture it helps to have a keen ear for language, and more specifically still, an ability to register the ways in which certain terms have entered or left the culture's everyday lexicon over the course of our lives.

For example, while terms like "fuck" and "suck," which were once reserved for the expression of our most savage emotions have gone banally mainstream, words like dignity and integrity, which embody timeless and universal ideals have become surprisingly scarce.

On those few occasions when it is uttered today, integrity is pretty much used as a synonym for honesty. While this is not wrong, I think it gives short shrift to the fullness of the concept lurking behind the word. Viewed etymologically, to have integrity is to be integral, that is, to be "one of a piece" and therefore largely devoid of internal fissures. In practice, this would mean being—or more realistically—assiduously seeking, to become the same person inside and out, to do what we think, and think about what we do.

Going back to the example of the dark room above, having true integrity would mean getting to a point where the sudden presence of the other person in the shadows would not disturb us because he or she would be seeing nothing in us that we would not want to be seen, or that we had not displayed openly on countless occasions in public settings.

There is, I believe, also an important existential correlate to this idea of integrity: the ability to enter into an active, honest and fruitful dialogue with what awaits us all, diminishment and death.

It is only through a constant and courageous engagement of the mystery of our own finiteness that we can calibrate the preciousness of time, and the fact that love and friendship may, in fact, be the only things capable of mitigating the angst induced by its relentless onward march.

There is nothing terribly new in what I have just said. Indeed, it has been a core, if not *the core*, concern of most religious traditions throughout the ages.

What is relatively new, however, is the full-bore effort by our economic elites and their attendant myth-makers in the press to banish these issues of mortality, and the moral postures they tend to channel us toward, from consistent public view. Why has this been done?

Because talk of transcendent concerns like these strike at the core conceit of the consumer culture that makes them fabulously wealthy: that life is, and should be, a process of endless upward expansion, and that staying on this gravity-defying trajectory is mostly a matter of making wise choices from among the marvelous products that mankind, in all its endless ingenuity, has produced, and will continue to produce, for the foreseeable future.

That the overwhelming majority of the world does not, and cannot, participate in this fantasy, and continues to dwell within the precincts of palpable mortality and the spiritual beliefs needed to palliate its day-to-day angst, never seems to occur to these myth-makers.

At times, it is true, the muffled screams of these "other" people manage to insinuate themselves into the peripheral reaches of our public conversation. But no sooner do they appear than they are summarily banished under a concerted rain of imprecation, containing words like terrorist, fascist, fundamentalist, anti-Western, anti-Semite, terms whose only real purpose is to drain their very real and logical complaints of any inherent moral claim.

And if, after belittling them and their concerns, they continue to squawk, we are not at all immune to killing them. And when we do, we don't even give them the minimal respect of having been fundamentally human, referring to them instead with terms like "collateral damage," and completely foreclosing the possibility that they might have died following a moral vision that might be at least as compelling and legitimate as our "right" to continue our flight from mortality by consuming the riches of the world as we see fit.

And it's not just the foreign others that we assiduously disappear from our visual and affective horizons.

Until the advent of consumerism, the elderly were seen as a precious resource, providing us all with much-needed wisdom and emotional ballast as we navigated life's difficulties. Now, however, we lock them and their encroaching decrepitude away so that they do not impinge upon our frenzied, self-directed pep-talks about the importance of staying forever young and highly productive.

So what eventually happens to a culture that has worked overtime to keep the key human realities of death and diminishment safely locked in the closet?

What happens is what is happening to us now in the midst of the Coronavirus crisis.

After so many years of essentially telling ourselves that mortality is a curable condition (for us), or one whose pain we can disappear (when we visit it on others), we find ourselves largely incapable of confronting the danger that the coronavirus now poses for us in a halfway rational and proportional fashion.

Am I saying that the coronavirus does not constitute a real threat? Absolutely not. It has produced a very real *health care crisis*—which is not necessarily the same as a huge *mortality crisis*—and obviously has the potential to kill lots of people.

But then again so does the planned poverty of our global capitalist system, so does the wonton pollution of our watersheds and the air we breathe, and so do wars of choice of the type this country has become so expert in waging over the last thirty years. And when we talk about the things I have just mentioned we are not navigating in the realm of potential calamity, as with the virus, but rather in that of starkly proven realities.

Indeed, coldly estimating loss of life, and making judgements about how much of it is required to achieve X or Y strategic goal is baked into our economic and military systems. And we've got the armies of actuarial scientists to prove this.

Just think of Madeleine Albright telling us unashamedly on *60 Minutes* that the death of 500,000 children as a result of American bombing of Iraq in the nineties "was worth it," or of Hillary Clinton chortling on screen about the death by bayonet thrust in the anus of Gaddafi, an event that led to the destruction of Libya and tens of thousands additional deaths across the entire northern half of Africa. Or the hundreds of thousands of deaths caused by the invasion of Iraq, or the current US-supported bombing of the wretchedly poor and cholera-ridden population of Yemen. If you are looking for a real crisis of mortality, I could point you in the right direction real quick.

And yet, when people propose putting the much lower sickness and mortality numbers (some 150,000 so far out of a world population of 7.8 billion) from the coronavirus in some sort of comparative perspective, and pose questions about whether bringing the entire Western social and economic order to its knees—with all that this portends for the already disadvantaged in terms of increased poverty and death, not to mention the ability of entrenched elites and the Deep State operators to take advantage of the resulting collapse—all of a sudden talking about death and its tradeoffs becomes a terrible breach of ethical sensibility.

Why the stark difference? How is it that 150,000 deaths—many which cannot even be definitively ascribed to the virus when considering the complex tangle of comorbidities presented by a clear majority of the victims—out of 7.8 billion people in 3 months "changes everything" when many, many more wholly avoidable deaths over many, many more years do not?

It's simple. Because untimely death is now potentially visiting "us"—those of us around the world who live in the pale of consumerist settlement with its ever attendant PR machine programmed to generate sales through fear—and not "them."

And if there is one thing that the ever youthful figure of *homo consumericus* absolutely won't put up with it is being forced to wrestle with mysteries of mortality in the way his ancestors did until a short time ago, and the way upwards of 6 billion other people on the planet still do every single day in our time.

17 April 2020

LET'S PRETEND

believe that retaining a vision of how you viewed the world in earlier moments of life is an essential element of navigating mindfully through the challenges of the present. It is only through a thoughtful and unsentimental rendering of how one's patterns of cognition have evolved—or not—that we can gain—or not—the capacity to face new challenges with equanimity, wisdom and confidence.

For example, I remember quite clearly how I viewed the world at age 6, how I tended to see people in rigidly binary terms, as either comforting or threatening, and that I imbued the former with infinite nurturing powers, and the latter, people like teachers and school principals, with the capacity to obliterate my being at the drop of a hat.

I also remember how single-minded I could be about things like candy and donuts, and how, when on their frequent Sunday dinner visits to our house my grandparents, uncles and aunts would bring one or both of these magic substances and place them in the kitchen, I had little ability to concentrate on anything else that was taking place in the house that day, and needless to say, on what might happen the day after.

I recently pondered how that same binary, monomaniacal and context-challenged 6-year-old brain might process the inputs we are currently receiving regarding the Covid crisis sweeping across our country and the world.

If I still thought with my 6-year-old brain, I would probably believe:

That I, along with my brothers and sisters and parents in their early 30s (remember I'm 6) are probably all in some sort of imminent mortal danger, despite the fact that statistics demonstrate quite forcefully that this is not even remotely the case for us, or indeed, the vast majority of people under 60.

That the now oft-repeated mantra that "saving lives" in the present is, as has always has been, a paramount goal of our society, and one, moreover, that has never been subject to unseemly and frankly unthinkable cost-benefit analyses like the ones actuaries from the Pentagon and health insurance companies, to name just two examples, regularly carry out concerning the trade-offs between deaths and the achievement of strategic and financial goals.

That the norm in the history of healthy societies is *not* to think first, and above all, about how to guarantee long-term opportunities for the young, but to do everything it takes, regardless of the damage it might do to those same young, to preserve the lives of the elderly who have already had the privilege of living long and, in the context of world history, very rich lives.

That to even posit the existence of this moral calculus, which has been present and actively contemplated by both individuals and collectives for millennia, and indeed, has impelled human beings to some of their greatest acts of heroism, is in and of itself a grave moral affront which, translated to Twitter-think, simply means that the speaker is a sadist that just wants to see the old suffer and die.

That the threat we are facing is "unprecedented" and is probably best compared the Spanish flu epidemic of 1918, when millions died when, in fact, the death rates in the US from Covid are much more comparable to standard, and generally unremarked upon, annual fatalities for pneumonia.

That scientific "experts" working out of a tradition that, among other things, proudly brought us Eugenics, lobotomies, thalidomide and agent orange, are always right and that to question their wisdom is tantamount to carelessly enabling massive death as well as declaring one's self a science-hating white supremacist. This despite the fact that the widely-heeded predictions of Covid deaths provided by one of the more supposedly esteemed members of the expert club, the British epidemiologist Neil Ferguson, have, so far, proven to be wildly off the mark.

That listening to anecdotes of horror from doctors immersed in an intense and exhausting treatment battles on the front lines in the country's relatively few heavy hit areas, or alternatively, highlighting distressing tales of the families heavily affected by the disease in the same places, is the best and most wise way to accurately assess the overall threat that Covid poses to the 330 million inhabitants of the US. You know, just like that age-old military practice of having the impressions of a corporal involved in fighting at the busiest point in the enemy front dictate the overall strategic vision of the General responsible for the overall design and implementation of the war plan.

That governments, most notably US, Italian and Israeli governments over the last seven or so decades, have never provoked, ignored or exaggerated threats to their own people, including some that have resulted the large-scale slaughter of innocent citizens, in order to frighten citizens into greater allegiance to established, if also increasingly discredited, centers of power.

That stay-at-home orders are about "keeping *us all* safe" when, in fact, they only protect the already protected and put the financially precarious, who are the majority of our population, in the position of either going hungry or working like dogs under bad conditions so that the rest of us can ride this thing out in relative comfort.

That the "Looting and Money Printing" bill proposed by Trump and passed nearly unanimously by Congress won't have very real mortal effects in the not-too-distant future and couldn't possibly put our children in an insurmountable fiscal hole.

That when the assuredly many more illnesses, deaths and suicides resulting from these measures materialize, the media, with its clear and demonstrated belief in the idea that each and every death is a tragedy that must not be glossed over or forgotten, will surely catalog them with the same breathless attention they have used to catalog the numbers of cases and deaths supposedly caused by the Covid virus.

That the same Trump bill will not result in the further concentration of wealth on Wall Street and in the offices of the major corporations at the expense of the already greatly debilitated middle class and small business sector.

That the desire to catch up to China in the day-to-day implementation of AI, something that is being greatly and rapidly facilitated by the present Covid-induced shift away from face to face retail to on-line entities like Amazon, does not have anything to do with issuing social isolation orders whose severity has no logical relation to the actual dimensions of the mortal threat posed by the virus.

That long-term planners in Washington never posit the belief that anything that further divides the EU is a good thing for the US as the West's pre-eminent hegemon, and that they never once thought about how engendering a particularly overwrought reaction to the Covid virus would inflame tensions within that multinational polity and thus further this goal while simultaneously making it more difficult to execute moves by the bloc to further conjoin its economic destiny to those of Russia and China.

That getting the majority of the people to believe in the dubious benefits of social distancing, which is to say a reflexive distrust of one's fellow citizens is not—in light of the fact that all revolutions, and even radical reform movements, begin with intimate meetings rooted in an essential trust of the other (the word conspire comes for the Latin term for "breathing together")—an enormous tactical triumph for a plutocratic class faced with an increasingly impoverished and restive population.

That the moving of so many more activities formerly carried out in the relative privacy of offices and classrooms to online platforms like Zoom, won't provide the already out of control privacy invasion industries, managed through a well-articulated condominium between Big Tech and the intelligence community, with the ability to know virtually everything about our thoughts on just about every possible subject, and that his information won't be used to try further blunt our ability to act, or even conceive of ourselves, as autonomous moral actors.

As you can see, facing complex issues like the Covid crisis with the unidimensional cognitive outlook of a 6-year-old is perilous business. Glad to know that when faced with constant media bombardment, most Americans, especially well-educated ones, almost never regress to thinking as I did in the presence of my grandmother's box of donuts.

8 May 2020

WHAT EVERYBODY "KNOWS"

For reasons related to the work of my wife, a handywoman deluxe, I have spent a good part of these last two weeks in a bucolic but economically depressed corner of the state of Connecticut. And since I'm an academic, with little ability at this point in my life to do carpentry, painting and other manual activities, I assumed the role of her errand man while there, something that put me in much greater contact that I usually have with non-college-educated people.

I took advantage of the opportunity to chat with everyone along the way. And not surprisingly, almost all these conversations quickly drifted towards the problem of managing Covid-19.

During these same days I participated in Zoom meetings and listservs with my faculty colleagues centering on how best to face the challenges presented by the coronavirus in the coming academic year.

I was quite struck by the stark contrast in both tone and content between the two sets of conversations.

In the academic forums, that is to say, assemblies made up of individuals belonging to what is possibly the most protected salaried class in the country, and who in recent months had held classes from the comfort of their homes in generally well-off neighborhoods, the expressions of fear were numerous and forceful. There was an almost religious solemnity in their voices when they talked of the "unprecedented" and "dangerous" nature of the Covid problem. And it goes without saying that none of the nearly two hundred doctors of philosophy gathered in these pow-wows expressed the slightest doubt that, given the self-evidently serious risks, we should do everything very, very carefully when we return to the classroom in the fall. And there were many among them who were dead set against returning to the classroom at all.

In the conversations with the men and women from the rural area, many of whom work in the building trades—and who during the lockdowns worked with others non-stop and usually without a mask—there were frequent expressions of skepticism, both about the true seriousness of the epidemiological problem, and about the necessity and effectiveness of the extreme measures being used to combat it. And when it came to their personal fears about the virus, the expressions of worry oscillated between little and none.

As the reader that I am of the "quality media" in the US and Europe, I know that the enlightened classes have a ready-made explanation for what I was seeing and hearing out in the country: these people's lack of education, along with their addiction to garbage media and religious superstition, leave them unable to truly perceive the magnitude of Covid's challenge to us as a society.

Okay. Except for the fact that it doesn't square with the content of my conversations at all.

Of my two groups of interlocutors, the only ones who spoke in minimally rigorous terms about the statistical reality of the problem – and therefore the real risk of mortality faced by ordinary people in the midst of the crisis – were the members of the more rural and less educated cohort.

With my academic colleagues almost everything said corresponded directly to the central tropes of the narrative pushed by Big Media, and the "evidence" they adduced to justify their sense of alarm consisted mostly of disturbing anecdotes, scarcely representative of the wider and statistically proven social realities.

At one point when discussing the health hazard the virus would pose to our students and ourselves were we to return to face-to-face instruction, I had the temerity to share with my colleagues CDC statistics on the death rate of Covid in the US nearly five months into the epidemic. Here they are:

a) In the 15-24 age range, a cohort that includes virtually all of our students, there had been 125 deaths out of a total of 44 million people. (.00028 percent death rate)

b) In the 15-65 age range, a cohort that includes a very high percentage of all those with a reason to be on campus there had been 19,913 deaths out of a total of 213 million people. (.0093 percent death rate)

The reaction? Complete silence.

No, the fact that the number of deaths in the population that studies and works at universities is about half of those who die annually in car accidents, had no effect on them. They continued to insist on the fact that the virus constitutes a very, very serious mortal danger to everyone in society.

One of the central presumptions of those in the educated class is that we are automatically much better equipped than the less educated to sort through the flows of information that surround us.

But what few from this group take into account is the possible effect that the desire for "cultural distinction" as Bourdieu phrased it, might have on our perceptions; that is, how our desire to see our superior cultural status in relation to the masses vividly confirmed, might cause us to suspend our highly developed sense of intellectual discernment. Or that whenever there are significant quantities of cultural prestige or money at stake in a debate, groupthink is just as real a possibility among the self-denominated wise as it is among the less educated.

This was just made clear by how easily the editors of *The Lancet* and *New England Journal of Medicine*, as well as most of their readers, completely swallowed an article on the therapeutic relationship between hydroxychloroquine and Covid based on completely false data sets.

Moreover, it seldom occurs to many people in the more educated classes that the great centers of social power might be successfully targeting them with highly calibrated campaigns of "perception management." And in the few cases in my experience when this is admitted as a theoretical possibility, my interlocutors express strong doubts that semiotic maneuvering of this kind could really work with people like them.

To paraphrase Sartre, in the world of the highly educated, the dupes of propaganda are always other people.

It seems to me, in contrast, that to live outside the imagined community of the well-educated is to inhabit a space marked by a persistent, if at the same time perhaps not always sophisticated, skepticism when it comes to judging how social power shapes the operative perceptions of social reality around us.

To inhabit this space is to understand almost instinctively that there will always be someone with more power than you trying to sell you a version of reality that facilitates the achievement of his or her vital interests much more than your own.

I think we can postulate the existence of an analogous dynamic in the area of perceiving and estimating life's risks. Again, in the world of the educated, it is assumed that our more intense training in sifting through large amounts of data gives us a generally superior ability to foresee and face the dangers that might derail our future plans.

But his general view omits an important fact: that those who excel in the art of calculating risks are usually those who have most often practiced it.

To be an independent carpenter with three children and with non-existent health insurance, or health insurance of very poor quality, is to necessarily develop a very refined nose for calculating risk.

It is also to become quite learned in the role that exaggerations and bluffing play in negotiations, especially when one is dealing with those possessing relatively more social power.

In contrast, we tenured university professors, with our guaranteed salaries, paid vacations and very solid health plans, do not have much need to engage in daily risk calculations, or to engage in frequent negotiations, with their inevitable tricks and distortions.

Perhaps this is why, when we well-protected and relatively well-paid professors do have to make a risk assessment or negotiate with power, we often to do it with the nervousness and credulity of the rookie.

In view of this, it seems legitimate to ask whether our desire as "educated" people, avid for the acquisition of cultural distinction, causes us to reflexively align ourselves with those whom our "quality media" have identified as the *non plus ultra* carriers of cultural capital.

And also to what extent our status as self-satisfied winners within the current social and information system might turn us into easy prey for well-designed perception management campaigns by centers of social and financial power on a social plane well above our own.

Otherwise, how can it be explained—if not as a product of solidarity between self-nominated sensible people ultra-confident in the *per se* superior quality of their own social tribe—that:

- Neil Ferguson, of Imperial College London, author of the egregiously wrong and now completely discredited Covid death predictions of last March—which of course were the trigger for the imposition of draconian lockdown policies around the world—is neither harshly criticized in the press or being threatened with legal actions?
- So many prestigious scientists from all over the world who made much less spectacular, but much more correct predictions about the probable epidemiological course of Covid-19, and treatment recommendations that were much more respectful of civil liberties (e.g. Ioannidis, Gupta, Giesecke, Bhakdi, Katz, Levitt, Wittkowski) appear so little in the mainstream media?
- Despite the evidence from other countries that has been available for some time that suggests that the closure of schools was unnecessary, and possibly even counterproductive from an epidemiological point of view, we see no large-scale movement against this cruel measure that will undoubtedly have large negative effects on the longitudinal development of millions of young people?

Given the heightened tensions of our time, perhaps I should take a moment as I close to explain what I am *not* saying:

- I am not saying that there is a society of rural and less educated wise people who always know more than educated people.
- I am not suggesting that Covid-19 is not real and that we do not have to take serious measures to combat it.
- I'm not saying that I don't believe in the scientific method or in scientists.

But what I am suggesting is that having more educational credentials is no guarantee against the danger of believing in stories that seriously distort our understanding of empirical facts.

If we are going to suggest that in less-schooled people there might be greater tendency to grant legitimacy to supernatural and spiritual powers, it seems fair to also suggest that in the credentialed classes today there is a tendency to uncritically accept the high-sounding abstractions of fellow credentialees, not so much on the rigor of their arguments, but on the basis of their perceived possession of cultural capital.

Am I suggesting that everything "the authorities" say is wrong? No. I'm simply underscoring the need to apply intellectual discernment on all pressing questions in a case-by-case manner, especially in relation to what everyone who is said to be smart thinks they already know about them.

27 June 2020

CONTRIVED SPECTACLES OF PROTECTING
AND CARING FOR THE PEOPLE

The 1970s marked an important turning point in the history of Western democracies. Having, for better or worse, led their populations to the obscene carnage of World War II, the US elites and those running their new vassal states in non-Communist Europe understood that it was in their interest to provide ordinary citizens of their societies with social and democratic rights and privileges seldom, if ever, seen in the history of humankind.

The effort was, for the most part, an enormous success. And therein lay precisely the problem: the masses who had grown up during the three decades following the war did not understand that the economic and governmental elites had no intention of allowing the regimes of supervised democracy of those years to evolve, over time, into true receptacles of the popular will.

The masses' inability to comprehend the implicit limits on their political agency was not a new problem. What was new were the restrictions on elite maneuverability imposed by the reality of the Cold War in this historical moment.

How could the elites resort to overwhelming violence, as they had traditionally done, to crush youthful rebellions in areas under their control when heavy-handedness of this type was precisely what they were criticizing day after day in their anti-communist propaganda?

An answer to this dilemma began to emerge in 1970s Italy with the so-called "Strategy of Tension." The method is as simple as it is diabolical and depends on the following reasoning: no matter how sclerotic, corrupt and discredited the existing regime of supervised democracy might be, people will seek refuge within its structures (thus giving those structures an instant dose of added legitimacy) when confronted with a generalized rise in levels of social fear.

How is this accomplished?

By planning and executing from within the government (or through non-governmental cutouts operating with the approval of key governmental factions) violent attacks against the population and attributing them to official enemies of the regime of supervised democracy.

And when the expected panic occurs (a panic magnified, of course, by the many controlled allies of the managed democracy in the press), the government puts itself forth as the beneficent protector of the lives of the citizenry.

Sound nutty, like a far out "conspiracy theory?" It is not.

What I have just explained – perhaps best exemplified by the terrorist attack on the Bologna railway station in 1980 – is extremely well-documented. The mystery is why so few people are familiar with these state crimes against their populations.

Is it a matter of fact-suppression by Big Media?

Or the reluctance of citizens themselves to grapple with the fact their rulers might be capable of such things? Probably both things simultaneously.

Once the 'democratic' challenges of the 1960s and 1970s were neutralized—in part by the ultra-cynical methods mentioned above, and in part by the strategic flaccidness of the activists themselves—the economic elites of the United States and its junior partners in Europe began to gallop as never before, consolidating during the 1980s and 1990s a level of control over the Western political class that would have been absolutely unthinkable in the first three decades of the post-war era.

The growing divide between the economic elites and the large mass of the population that resulted from these changes was hidden during the 1990s by, among other things, the cyber revolution (with its corresponding financial bubbles and quotas of mental distraction) and by the enthusiasm arising from the collapse of communism and the apparent consolidation of the European Union.

But if there is one thing that elites—be they financial, clerical, or military—have always understood, it is that no system of ideological control lasts forever. And even less so in the age of consumerism, characterized, as Bauman reminds us, by the compulsive search for new future sensations, on the one hand, and rampant forgetfulness, on the other.

In this new, more 'liquid' context, a single terrifying event—such as the government-approved Bologna massacre—has a much more limited domesticating effect than before.

Why?

Because, in an environment increasingly dominated by forgetting and the headlong search for new and different consumerist sensations, the disciplinary effects of a singular shock to the social system will endure for a much more limited time within the brain of the average citizen.

And it was in this context, in the late 1990s, that the strategists of the United States and its European servants, collaborating in the context of their well-financed "Atlanticist" networks, began to adapt their "perception management" tactics to the new cultural reality.

How?

By turning consumerism's obligatory forgetfulness, which they had initially viewed as a hindrance to the process of imposing social discipline, into their great ally.

Now instead of administering small shocks of limited temporal and geographical effect upon the citizenry, they would create large social disruptions, the disorienting effects of which would then be bolstered from time to time by smaller thematically-related campaigns of fright.

They wanted, in effect, to put into practice what seemed unreal and absolutely dystopian when Guy Debord described it in 1967: an all-enveloping and energy-draining *spectacle* that while constant in terms of the amount of social space it occupies, regularly changes its plastic, visual and verbal forms, a spectacle that for all its omnipresence in the minds of the populace, often has only a very tenuous relationship with the empirical material realities of their day-to-day lives.

When, during the last decade of the 20th century, talk began in Atlanticist military and intelligence circles of "Full-spectrum dominance," most observers understood it mainly in terms of classical military capabilities; that is, the ability of the US and NATO to physically destroy the enemy in the widest possible variety of situations.

However, over time, it has become clear that the most dramatic progress made under this doctrine is in the field of information control and perception management.

I do not claim to understand all the operational realities behind the attacks on the Twin Towers in 2001. What I am sure of, however, is that the spectacle organized in reaction to these acts of destruction was by no means spontaneous or improvised.

The most obvious proof of this is how, just six weeks after the attacks, the US Congress passed the Patriot Act, a 342-page piece of legislation which was nothing more and nothing less than a compendium of all the curbs on basic civil rights that the harshest elements of the US Deep State had been dreaming about enacting for several decades.

The careful observer of the country's information environment will find many more indicators of a surprising degree of coordination in the media treatment of the 2001 attacks, a pattern of behaviors that we might do well to reacquaint ourselves with as we try and make sense of the Covid phenomenon.

Below are some of the more salient features of the spectacle that was generated in response to the attacks that took place in New York nearly two decades ago.

1. The very early and constant repetition in the media that the attack was an absolutely "unprecedented" phenomenon in the history of the country, and quite possibly in the world.

Those of us who study history know that there are very few occurrences that cannot be compared to others in the past, and that, moreover, it is precisely this practice of making transtemporal analogies that endows history with its great social value.

Without this ability to compare, we would always find ourselves trapped in the emotional sensations and pains of the present, without the ability to relativize what is happening to us, which is of course essential if we are to react to life's difficulties with wisdom and proportion.

On the other hand, who might profit by having citizens living in a timeless bubble of trauma, convinced that no one else in history has suffered in ways they are currently suffering? I think the answer is obvious.

2. The constant repetition in the media, from the first moment following the attacks, that this day would "change everything."

How can we know in the first moment following this event or any other that our lives will be fundamentally and inexorably changed? In addition to being very complex and full of surprises, life is also us and our combined will to shape it. And while there is no doubt that we have never had absolute control over the fate of our collective life, we have also never been mere spectators in its development.

That is, unless and until we decide to relinquish that responsibility. In whose interest is it to induce in us a feeling of futility or a lack of agency regarding the future? Who benefits by convincing us that we will not be able to sustain or recover long-cherished elements of our lives? In whose interest is it that we abandon the idea that we can be something more than mere spectators in the drama before us? I suspect it is someone other than most of us.

3. TINA or "There is no alternative."

When a country, especially a very rich country with many tentacles in global business and worldwide institutions, is attacked, it has many tools at its disposal and, therefore, many possible ways to react to the event.

For example, had it wanted to, the US could have easily used the events of September 11th to showcase how justice could be achieved through cooperation between legal teams and police forces from countries around the world, a position that had numerous eloquent adherents within the US and abroad.

But none of them appeared on the screens of the nation's viewers. No, from the outset, the media spoke relentlessly, not about the moral and strategic advantages or disadvantages of a military attack, but about its impending operational details. Almost from the moment the Towers fell, commentators spoke of a massive military attack on someone, with the same naturalness one uses to observe that the sun rises in the morning. We were told constantly, in large and small ways, that there was no alternative to this plan of action.

4. Create a body of television commentators who, with very slight variations in style, political affiliation and policy proposals, subscribe to all the basic assumptions mentioned above.

In fact, when a careful study of these pundits is done, we find frankly terrifying levels of organizational inbreeding among them. As Thomas Friedman, one of the best-known members of this gang of so-called experts said in an unguarded moment of candor in a conversation with Israeli journalist Ari Shavit in 2003:

"I could give you the names of 25 people (all of whom are at this moment within a five-block radius of this office) who, if you had exiled them to a desert island a year and a half ago, the Iraq war would not have happened."

It was only members of this group, or their designated spokespersons, who had the "right" to explain the "reality" of the post-9/11 crisis to the country's citizens.

5. To create, with the full indulgence of the big media, a regime of public punishment for those who were opposed to the prescriptions of the small group of neocon experts mentioned above.

For example, when Susan Sontag, perhaps the most notable female American intellectual of the second half of the twentieth century, wrote an article harshly criticizing the US government's violent and clearly disproportionate reaction to the attacks, she was severely reprimanded and shamed throughout the media. A little while later, Phil Donahue, whose talk show boasted MSNBC's highest audience share at the time, was fired for having invited too many people with anti-war views to his program. This last statement is not speculation. It was made clear in an internal company document leaked to the press shortly after he lost his job.

6. The seamless and non-sensical substitution of one supposedly important "reality" for another.

What was officially an attack by a group of Saudis became a pretext for the invasion of Afghanistan, and then Iraq. Extremely logical, right? Obviously not.

But it is also obvious that the authorities understood that, under the influence of the spectacle, with its constant dance of traumatic images, logical thinking can be effectively suspended in the minds of many citizens.

7. The invention and repeated deployment 'floating" or "empty" signifiers—emotionally evocative terms presented without the contextual armature needed to imbue them with any stable and unequivocal semantic value—designed to spread and sustain panic in society.

The classic examples of this were the constant mentions of WMDs and terror warnings in the form of multicolored thermometers with various "temperatures" of risk generated by Homeland Security beginning—what a coincidence—precisely at the moment the original psychological shock of the 9-11 attacks was beginning to fade.

An attack where? By whom? A threat according to what sources? We were never clearly told.

And that was precisely the point: to keep us vaguely frightened, and therefore much more willing to accept any security measures imposed by our "protective parents" in government.

Might there be a relationship between the set of propaganda techniques I have just sketched out and the spectacle currently being generated in relation to the Covid-19 phenomenon?

I can't be sure. But in the interest of stimulating a more in-depth analysis of the subject, I will pose a few questions.

Is Covid-19 really an unprecedented threat when we consider, for example, the death tolls of the Asian flu of 1957 or the Hong Kong flu of 1967-68?

Can we really say, in light of the levels of mortality in many countries of the world in recent months that Covid 19 is a virus against which human bodies have no known defense, and before which, therefore, the classic solution of herd immunity has no validity?

Why should everything change with this epidemic? Epidemics have been a constant companion of human beings throughout their history on Earth. If the epidemics of 1918, 1957 and 1967-68 did not "change everything," why should it be the case this time? Could it simply be that there are very large centers of power that, for reasons of their own, might want "everything to change" this time around?

Do you really think it is a mere coincidence that, in a world where pharmaceutical companies move obscene amounts of money, and where the WHO and the GAVI depend quite heavily for funding on the money of a man obsessed with creating mass vaccination programs, the corporate media has systematically "forgotten" about the millennial human capacity to create defenses against new viruses? And that nearly all public discussions of solutions revolve—in true TINA fashion—exclusively around the development of a vaccine?

Do you really think that your media has allowed you to hear a wide range of expert opinions on how to respond to the epidemic? There are quite a few scientists of great prestige around the world who, from the beginning, have made clear that they do not accept the notion that Covid represents an "unprecedented" threat to human beings.

Do you find it strange that none of these people are regularly asked to appear in Big Media?

Have you examined the possible links to, and possible financial dependency upon, the WHO, GAVI and other pro-vaccine entities among those most frequently appearing in the media?

Do you think it is a mere coincidence that Sweden, which did not yield to the enormous pressure to curtail the basic freedoms of its citizens over Covid, and which has had *per capita* mortality levels below Italy, Spain, France, the UK and Belgium, has been the constant target of criticism from the prestige media, starting with *The New York Times*?

Do you find it at all odd that the head of the anti-Covid effort in that country, Anders Tegnell, has been the subject of very aggressive interrogations in his contacts with journalists? This, while walking epidemiological disasters, and cheerful destroyers of fundamental rights like Fernando Simón (Spain's chief adviser on the epidemic), and other similar authoritarian arsonists like Governor Cuomo of New York State are treated with docile respect by most scribes?

Does it seem normal to you that, in a dramatic reversal of historically predominant moral logic, the press harshly questions those who most want to preserve the social fabric and the existing rhythms of life while they lionize those who most seek to disrupt it?

Does it not seem a bit strange to you that the original pretext for curtailing the fundamental rights of citizens—reducing the curve of infections so as not to overload the health system—disappeared suddenly and without a trace from our public discourse only to be replaced, as death rates were steadily falling, with the journalistic obsession with the number of "new cases?"

Does it seem at all odd that no one now remembers or talks about the fact that many experts, including Fauci and the WHO before June 12, spoke about the essential uselessness of mask-wearing in relation to a virus like this?

Do you find it strange that almost no one talks about the report by the BBC's Deb Cohen which said that the WHO changed their experts' finding on the essential uselessness of masks in June under heavy political pressure?

Have you considered the possibility that the term "case" may be a floating or empty sign par excellence, in the sense that the media seldom, if ever, provides us the contextual information we need to turn it into a meaningful indicator of the real dangers we face with the virus?

If you accept the premise, which as we said before is eminently debatable, that Covid-19 is not like any other virus in human history and therefore the only way we have to eradicate it is with a vaccine, then an increase in "cases" is clearly bad news.

But what if, as many prestigious experts who have not been able to appear in the major media think, the concept of herd immunity is perfectly applicable to the phenomenon of Covid-19? In this context, an increase in cases, combined with a steady decline in the number of deaths at the same time (the reality, in the vast majority of countries in the world today), is, in fact, very good news.

Don't you find it strange that this possibility is not even mentioned in the media?

Beyond all this there is the indisputable fact that the vast number of those infected with Covid-19 are not in any mortal danger whatsoever. That is not just my opinion. It is the opinion of Chris Whitty, Chief Medical Officer for England, Chief Medical Adviser to the UK Government, Chief

Scientific Adviser at the Department of Health and Social Care (UK) and Head of the National Institute for Health Research (UK) who, on May 11th, said of the virus:

> "The great majority of the people will not die from it..... Most people, uh well, a significant proportion of people, will not get this virus at all at any point in the epidemic which is going to go on for a long period of time. Of those that do, some of them will get the virus without even knowing it, they will have a virus with no symptoms at all, asymptomatic carriage. Of those that get symptoms, the great majority, probably 80 per cent, will have mild or moderate disease. It might be bad enough for them to go to bed for a few days, not bad enough for them to go to the doctor. An unfortunate minority will have to go as far as hospital. The majority of them will just need oxygen and then leave the hospital. And then a minority of those will have to go to severe and critical care. And some of those, sadly, will die. But that's a minority, one percent, or possibly even less than one percent overall. And even in the highest risk group, this is significantly less than 20 percent, i.e. the great majority of the people, even the very highest groups, if they catch this virus will not die. And I really wanted to make that point really clearly."

Do you find it odd that Whitty's clear and comforting statement was not broadcast more widely?

Unfortunately, there are many people, including some who see themselves as quite sophisticated, who, immersed in the consumptive logic of the spectacle, refuse to consider that what the US leadership class did after 9/11 attacks might not have been spontaneous and logical reaction to the acts committed by terrorists, but rather a means of achieving long-cherished goals of the country's Deep State apparatus.

Similarly, there are many people, including local and state politicians of goodwill, who can only let themselves think that what is being done in reaction to the Covid-19 phenomenon is rooted in a sincere and pure desire to save the country from a life-threatening disease.

Observing this latter group, one can only conclude that deep within the secular culture that most of these people subscribe to, there exists a religious impulse, anchored in a desire for improbable childishly imagined salvific outcomes, that is every bit as strong as that which existed in the supposedly primitive cultures of yesteryear.

3 August 2020

NO ONE COULD HAVE KNOWN?

Ready for another rendition of the "no one could have known" routine made famous by all the self-proclaimed patriots who shamelessly went along with the Neocons' pre-planned and lie-supported destruction of the Middle East nearly two decades ago?

As in "no one could have known" that by shutting down life as we know it to focus obsessively on a virus mostly affecting a relatively small number of people at the end of their lives, we probably would:

1. Cause economic devastation and hence excess deaths, suicides, divorces and depressions in much larger numbers than those provoked by the virus.
2. Provide an already monopolistic and predatory online retailing establishment with competitive advantages in terms of capital reserves and market share that will make it virtually impossible at any time in the near or medium future for the country and the world's small and even medium-sized businesses to ever catch up to them. And that this will plunge huge sectors of the worldwide economy into serf-like ruin, with all that this portends in terms of additional death and human suffering.
3. Cause greatly increased misery and countless additional deaths in the so-called Global South where many people, rightly or wrongly, depend on the consumption patterns of the relatively fortunate sit-at-homers in countries like ours to make it through the week.
4. Destroy much of what was attractive about urban life as we know it and lead to a real estate collapse of extraordinary proportions, turning even our few remaining showplace cities into crime-ridden reserves of ever more desperate people.

5. Force state and local governments, already struggling before the crisis, and unable to print money at will as the Feds can, to cut their already insufficient budgets at a time when their broke and stressed constituents need those services more than ever.
6. Push "smart" monitoring of our lives, already intolerable for anyone still clinging to memories of freedom in the pre-September 11th world, to the point where most people will no longer understand what people used to know as privacy, intimacy or the simple dignity of being left alone.
7. Train a generation of children to be fearful and distrustful of others from day one, and to view bending to diktats "to keep them safe," (no matter how empirically dubious the actual threat to them might be), rather than the courageous pursuit of joy and human fullness, as the key goal in life.

We will also no doubt be told that no one could have imagined or known at the time:

> That government officials often make policy on the basis of information they know to be largely unsubstantiated or flat-out false, and work on the premise that by the time the few conscientious researchers out there get around looking past the hype to debunk these bogus storylines, the repressive structures that were put into place on the basis of the false narrative will have been normalized, and thus be in no danger of being dismantled.
>
> That our educational institutions, already failing miserably in the essential democratic task of educating the young to engage in productive conflict with those whose ideas are different than their own, will only further promote dehumanization of "the other" through ever-greater reliance on the disembodied practices of remote learning. And that this, in turn, will only encourage the further growth of the cancellation approach to "coping" with new and challenging ideas.
>
> That further fomenting the alienated and alienating educational practices mentioned above will make it easier than it

already is for our oligarchs to enhance their already obscene levels of control over our daily lives and long-term destinies through divide and rule tactics.

That, according to the Institute for Democracy and Election Assistance (IDEA), fully two-thirds of elections scheduled to be held since February have been postponed due to Covid. And that this does much to accustom citizens and populations to the idea that one of their few remaining democratic rights can essentially be taken away on the basis of bureaucratic whims, creating a dangerous "new normal" that obviously favors the interests of established centers of power.

That Sweden and other countries developed much more proportionate, culture-saving and dignity-saving ways to live safely and much more fully with the virus.

That Anthony Fauci has a well-documented tendency to see every health problem as being amenable to expensive pharmaceutical solutions, even when other less intrusive, less expensive, and equally effective therapies are available.

That the recent history of using vaccines to fight respiratory infections has been ineffective when not grotesquely counterproductive.

That during the first half of the 20th century the infectious disease of polio was a constant danger, culminating in 1952 with a devastating toll of 3,145 deaths and 21,269 cases of paralysis in a US population of 162,000,000, almost all of the victims being children and young adults. The danger then to the under-24 population (some 34 million) of being infected (0.169 percent) paralyzed (0.044 percent) or killed (0.0092 percent) far outstripped in percentages and, obviously, severity, anything Covid is doing to the same age group. And yet there was no talk of blanket school closures, canceled high school, college and pro sports or, needless to say, lockdowns or masking for the entire society.

That the world lost some 1.1 million people in the 1957-58 Asian flu epidemic (more than the present Covid number of 760,000), with some 116,000 in the US (0.064 percent of the population) and the world similarly did not stop.

That the Hong Kong flu of 1968-69 killed between 1 and 4 million worldwide and some 100,000 in the US (0.048 percent of population killed) and that life similarly was not stopped. Indeed, Woodstock took place in the middle of it.

That the decisions to get on with life in all of these cases were probably not the result, as some today might be tempted suggest, of a lack of scientific knowledge or lesser concern for the value of life, but rather a keener understanding in the more histori-cally-minded heads of that time that risk is always part of life and that aggressive attempts to eliminate this most ubiquitous human reality can often lead to severe unwanted consequences.

That there were many prestigious scientists, including Nobel Prize winners, who told us as early as March 2020 that this virus, while new, would in greater or lesser measure behave much like all viruses before it and fade away. And, therefore, the best way to deal with it was to let it run its course while protecting the most vulnerable people in society and letting everyone else live their lives.

That significant information platforms banned or sidelined the views of these high-prestige scientists, while aggressively circu-lating the words of proven jokers like Neil Ferguson at Imperial College London, whose stupid and alarmist predictions of Covid mortality (the latest in a career full of stupid and alarmist, but not coincidentally, Pharma-friendly predictions), gave politicians the pretext for setting in motion perhaps the most aggressive experiment in social engineering in the history of the world.

That just as the levels of mortality from the virus were dimin-ishing rapidly in the late spring and early summer of 2020, thus raising hope for a much-needed return to normality, there was seamless bait and switch in the major media from a discourse centering on the logical and laudable goal of "flattening the curve" to one centering on the absurdly utopian (and not coin-cidentally vaccine-oriented) goal of eliminating new "cases."

That having the news media focus narrowly and obsessively on the growth of "cases" when 99 percent+ of them are completely non-life-threatening was journalistic malpractice of the highest order, comparable to, if not exceeding in its sinister effect that which was generated by the media's wholly unsubstantiated talk of mushroom clouds and WMDs two decades ago.

That as numerous existing and emerging studies seem to demonstrate hydroxychloroquine is, when combined with other similarly affordable drugs, a safe and rather effective early-stage treatment for Covid 19.

That the negative studies on hydroxychloroquine effectiveness published at two of the most prestigious medical journals in the world The *Lancet* and the *New England Journal of Medicine*, and which were adduced time and again at a key moment in the early debate of possible Covid treatments to debunk the drug's effectiveness, were found to be based on forged data sets. (see earlier entry on how power centers play the game of perception lag with false information to achieve long-term structural changes).

That suggesting world-class professional athletes in their 20s and 30s, or even their less talented and less fit high school and college counterparts, were running a risk of mortal consequences in even minimal numbers by playing in the midst of the Covid spread was, in light of known age-related numbers on the disease's lethality, at best ridiculous and, at worst, a very cynical fear-mongering ploy.

Repeat after me, *"no one could have possibly known these things"* and then check your screen to see, as citizens of Oceania, whether you are supposed to be worried this week about the threat from Eurasia or Eastasia.

22 August 2020

THE MERCHANTS OF MORAL PANIC

I n his famous *Understanding Media* published in 1964 Marshall McLuhan used the term "moral panic" to refer to the fright experienced by certain cultural elites when confronted by the written text's loss of influence before emergent forms of electronic media.

A few years later, Stanley Cohen, a British sociologist born in South Africa, made McLuhan's phrase the focus of his study on the tensions between "mods" and "rockers"—two youth sub-groups of the working class—in British society.

Cohen highlights the key role played by "moral entrepreneurs" from the media in greatly overstating the degree to which the skirmishes between these groups of impoverished youth could and would endanger social peace. He further argues that these sustained campaigns of exaggeration had the effect of turning these lower-class beings into "folk devils"; that is, "a visible reminder of what we were not to be," a formulation which, in turn, bolstered the existing values of bourgeois society.

The British historian Helen Graham has made very good use of the concept of moral panic in her analyses of the treatment of women in the early years of the Franco regime (1939-1975). The liberation of women on many social fronts during the Republic (1931-39) had, in many ways, shaken the pillars of Spain's then still very traditional society. Upon winning the Civil War and establishing the dictatorship, the Francoists greatly exaggerated supposed moral transgressions of Republican women to legitimize the repression they were using to return them to their "natural" place in the social order.

No matter how aggressive and cocksure both the entrepreneurs of moral panic in the media and their acolytes in the general population might at first glance appear to be, the main driver of their actions is always the spirit of defeat; that is, the consciousness of having lost the level of social control that they thought was their perpetual inheritance.

When dominant social elites encounter phenomena that not only disturb them, but do not even fit minimally within the phenomenological frameworks about reality they have engineered for themselves and others, they invariably respond with coercion, and if that does not work, eventually with violence.

As heirs of a century and a half of intermittent, but globally positive, progress in the attainment of individual rights (and the consequent deconstruction of the old clerical and social class privileges), it is logical that many of us tend to associate the phenomenon of moral panic with the political right. And there are many reasons for doing so. From Le Bon, and his theories about the dangerous nature of the masses in the 1800s, to today's Trumps, Erdogans, Bolsonaros, Abascals (Spain) and Orbans, the right has repeatedly resorted to moral panic to strengthen the foundations of its social power.

But I think it is a very big mistake to assume that the use of moral panic is strictly a right-wing phenomenon.

Moral panic is, in fact, a tool available to supporters of any social group possessed, on the one hand, of a substantial level of anguish over the relative loss of its social hegemony, and on the other, of the media connections needed to mount a sustained campaign to demonize nonconformists.

The spectrum of ideologies we call "left-wing" was born to do one thing above all others: to carry out a revision (radical in some branches of the ideological current, not so much in others) of the relations of economic power in society. It was not, as the study of European and South American anarchism clearly shows us, that activists working under the various acronyms of the left had no interest in pursuing a revision of other codes of social power. It was that they generally saw the revision of these other social codes as dependent on the reasonably satisfactory resolution of the economic question.

The widespread popularity and growth of left-wing parties in Europe in the first three or four decades after World War II was the result, above all, of this emphasis on the creation of economic structures designed to redistribute wealth in a much more equitable way than had ever been the case.

That was until a new version of so-called free market economics broke into the high precincts of government in the late 1970s and early 1980s, a development that seems to have taken the rulers of the then still dominant Leftist parties almost completely by surprise.

The inability to react quickly to new realities or to foresee the future is not a sin. What is morally reprehensible, however, is to pretend over time that the world has not changed, and that these changes do not seriously affect the people who are voting for you year after year.

And what is truly disgusting are the attempts by these once dominant Leftist parties to try and cover up their serial stupor and laziness in the face of the often rapacious financialization of the economy over the last four decades by mounting campaign after campaign of moral panic.

When viewed in the light of its own original postulates the Left has failed miserably in carrying out its appointed task of checking and eventually reversing Big Finance's frequent humiliation of millions of common people.

But instead of admitting their failure and convening broad and robust conversations within their ranks and with their political opponents about the most effective new ways to fight for economic justice, they insult us with absurd linguistic restrictions (which are, by definition, also cognitive constraints) and endless stories about the horrible and ever immoral authoritarians of the Right.

This, as if removing "offensive words" from our vocabularies was the key to pulling millions out of misery and precariousness, or as if the growing popularity of the so-called authoritarian leaders had nothing to do with many people's sense of having been abandoned to the depredations of often rigged markets while being preached to about the inherent wrongness of their long-standing moral codes. Or as if these so-called "Leftist" parties in power actually had any concrete plans to mitigate the toxic influence of Big Finance, Big Pharma and Big Tech.

This 30-year "Leftist" lurch toward morally charged bullying designed to cover up the movement's epic failure to ensure the freedom and dignity of common people has reached truly delirious proportions during the Covid crisis.

This social sector's cultural impresarios are no longer content, as they were for so long, to try and induce conformity and obedience through sneering and derision.

No, they are now demanding that we offer up our bodies and those of our children to them, not as they claim, or in some cases might even absurdly believe, as a way of ensuring the safety of all, but as a palpable sign of our conformity with their idea of how the world should really be.

Through these tactics—and I think it is important we are frank with ourselves about this—they have managed to put us all, like the mods and rockers in 1960s Great Britain, on the defensive.

And we must also be frank about the fact that we are now witnessing nothing more and nothing less than a campaign of naked aggression against those who refuse to pay physical homage, offering a blood sacrifice if you will, to an idea of moral correctness rooted, at the very best, in shambolic logic.

So how can and should we respond to this reality? First it is imperative that we recognize and accept that we are up against a sustained campaign of verbal cum physical violence.

Very few of us like conflict and thus often go to great lengths to minimize and/or paper over its existence in our lives. Moreover, our current consumerist culture, rooted in a one-must-always-be-cool trans-actionalist ethos, only enhances this natural human tendency.

This reticence, in turn, serves to embolden our opponents and, perhaps more importantly, generates paralysis in many of us for, as a very wise healer once said to me, "Anger turned inward becomes depression, and with depression comes an inability to exercise agency in life."

So, as primitive and untasteful as it may sound—especially to those of us socialized in the higher reaches of intellectual culture—we must begin to embrace our anger and to focus it like a satellite-killing laser beam against the only things that our opponents currently have going for them in the fight for public opinion: their false aura of moral supe-riority and the preemptive ability, thanks to massive media collusion, to frame the terms of the debate.

We must not only rationally pick apart their laughable distortions of science, but also directly challenge their self-appointed "right" to decide what are and should be the social priorities for each and every wonderfully unique individual in society, as well as the questions that can be asked about the reality of the problem before us.

An important element of this last approach is to *never* accept the terms of the debate as they have framed it. To attempt, for example, to preemptively distance ourselves from the question of "conspiracy theories" around Covid is, in effect, to ratify on the epistemological level the idea that there are trains of thought that can and should be summarily dismissed, a posture that is absolutely central to their efforts at control, and one that we as insurgents cannot afford to legitimize.

I mentioned above that most of us will do quite a lot to avoid flat-out interpersonal conflict. That is true.

But it is also true that most people have a deep abhorrence of bullying and self-interested moral hypocrisy. We thus must be relentless in high-lighting this essential aspect of those stage-managing the Covid crisis.

Though most have tried to forget it, I remember quite clearly the days and months after September 11th when the mainstream press corps tittered like star-struck schoolchildren before the moralizing lies of Donald Rumsfeld, with *People Magazine* going so far as to include him in its "Sexiest Man Alive" issue.

When the unindicted war criminal died recently, however, his former cheerleaders were nowhere to be found, nor were they asked to atone for their role in constructing and maintaining the grotesque myth of his wisdom and concern for human values.

Why?

Because too many of us who knew better failed to forcefully confront him and his fellow warmongers and their press enablers in real time.

And thus he was allowed, McArthur-style, to "just fade away."

Let's resolve now to not let the Covid hysterics merely fade away, using our imaginations to find ways of making it as uncomfortable as we possibly can for these merchants of moral panic to continue to practice their craft, and exercise their magisterium over public opinion.

Our children and grandchildren will, I think, be grateful for our effort.

30 October 2020

IF RATIONALITY EVER RETURNS...

● ● ● Historians will marvel at the attempted suicide of Euro-American culture set in motion by a virus that killed roughly 3 of 1,000 people that contracted it, the vast majority of whom were over 75 and with already compromised health.

They will wonder and marvel at how the culture of consumerism suddenly sapped most in this cultural space of the basic desire to live as freely as possible in the face of the nemesis that has always stalked each and every inhabitant of the earth: death.

They will wonder and marvel at how the inhabitants of this world, who as recently as seven decades before had responded to infinitely greater threats to their existence with hope and optimism, and subsequently, with the construction of perhaps the freest and most comfortable culture that humanity had ever seen, suddenly decided to close up shop and terminate that project before this puny scare.

They will examine the superstitions that made them do it, superstitions as absurd as the wearing of garlic necklaces in previous times—but presented dishonestly and hubristically in the name of science—and wonder at the astonishing inversion of basic social aspirations and thought processes.

They will, I suspect, ultimately conclude that by garrisoning ourselves in cubicles of material opulence, or the often unsuccessful pursuit thereof, we fatally unhinged ourselves from the contemplation of, and engagement with, the only things that life has ever been about in any enduring way: love, friendship, survival and the pursuit of joy within the often difficult trials of this existence, and that we simply gave up, exhausted and devoid of imagination and vital ambition.

13 November 2020

THE CASEDEMIC AND THE NORMALIZATION
OF ARBITRARY DETENTION

One of the great civic and political controversies in New York City during the last few decades centered on stop and frisk, the administrative policy that allowed a police officer, or a group of police officers, to stop, question, and if he or she liked, to physically search anyone whom they believed might be a threat to public safety.

It was instituted by former mayor Rudy Giuliani in response to a wave of media hysteria concerning the allegedly widespread existence of ultra-violent black and Hispanic gangs following the case of the so-called Central Park Five in 1989. It was widely practiced until 2013, when Judge Shira Sheindlin declared it unconstitutional. The following year, when Bill di Blasio was elected mayor, he ordered that all similar police practices be ended.

During those nearly two decades, more than 80 percent of those stopped were black or Hispanic, and in more than 85 percent of the cases, none of these searches resulted in any legal charges.

In light of these facts, it is not surprising that the progressive political elements of the city, and indeed much of the country, applauded the derogation of the program.

The victory over stop and frisk reaffirms one of the most basic principles of the legal systems emerging from early modernity and the Enlightenment: that no matter how disturbing to some the physical appearance or manner of dress of an individual might be, that person can only be deprived of his liberty if there is concrete and verified evidence of the consummated commission of a crime, or of a very clearly suggested desire to commit one.

One of the most important corollaries of this principle is that, in the case of serious doubts about the guilt or potential culpability of the individual in question, the state is obligated to default to the presumption of innocence and thus citizen freedom.

Though it seems absurd to have to repeat this, epidemics are only of public interest insofar as they a) kill people – with all the horrible side effects that entails – and b) unduly burden the society's health systems.

Talking about "cases"—a term which until the spring of 2020 was only used in medicine to talk about people who showed verifiable symptoms of a disease according to a doctor's diagnosis—is, it would seem, only useful, in public discourses about an epidemic if there is a stable, constant and predictable relationship between the number of discovered "cases" and the two essential issues mentioned above.

Lacking such a precise calibration, it is the equivalent, as I have argued elsewhere, to an empty or floating sign in linguistics; that is, a term that while it can suggest certain hazy emotional or intellectual connotations, does little or nothing to advance our precise empirical understanding of the social problems before us.

Despite this, I get the impression that almost all my friends and most everyone working in the media seem to believe that the daily number of cases reported is, in and of itself, a clear and unequivocal sign of the level of mortal danger we face with the virus.

Yet this is clearly not so.

Let's go to the CDC's official figures on the number of deaths per week since the beginning of the crisis. We can see clearly that the mortality of the epidemic reached its peak in mid-April, 2020 (with 17,087 deaths) and that, despite some small increases in August, it has stabilized at a level between 4,500 and 5,500 deaths the week, in a country of 330 million people; a mortality level just a little above what Covid must have to maintain its official status as declared epidemic. However, we can see that throughout this period the number of cases has continued to increase.

A very similar fatality curve – very high in the spring and consider-ably more stable and low since about May – is found, with only slight variations in almost all countries of the Northern Hemisphere. And this, notwithstanding the considerable differences between the countries in regard to the severity of alleged containment measures such as lockdowns and masking.

And in no country – despite the constant dire predictions, and again regardless of the level of social restrictions imposed – has the second wave had an effect on mortality even remotely similar to that caused by the virus in the spring. Seeing this evidence, several scientists of established prestige like Michael Yeadon have suggested that the Covid pandemic, understood in the classic sense of an event marked by mass mortality, is over.

"How can you be so stupid? I can hear my friends say, "The cases are increasing every day."

Yes, it's true. And other important facts are also true:

1. If you do more tests, you will get more positives.
2. The vast majority of people who test positive are asymptomatic or have very mild symptoms that do not require hospitalization or medical attention.
3. As clearly shown in a large-scale study done in Wuhan and published in *Nature* very recently, there was almost no transmission to other people by asymptomatic people in that huge Chinese city.
4. PCR tests – whose inventor, Nobel laureate Cary Mullis, said in an interview were not able to accurately detect the indication of the presence of live diseases – are notorious for their ability to generate false positives. For example, the US FDA says that the Covid PCR tests should be used at forty cycles (ct) or more of amplification. The problem, as Anthony Fauci himself said in July of 2020 "If get a cycle threshold of thirty-five or more, the chances of it being replication competent (accurate) are minuscule."

This is why certain people are saying that we are no longer suffering from a pandemic but from a casedemic. And there are some, possessing superb academic credentials, who think that it is not exactly a coincidence.

For example, according to the esteemed German immunologist Sucharit Bhakdi, members of the German government's task force on Covid spoke openly in March 2020 about the need to foment social panic in order to get the population's consent to new social restrictions. Citing a leaked document from the meeting (later dubbed the Panic Paper) Bhakdi notes how the group made a strategic decision to harp on the number of infections rather than the number of deaths. Why? Because the number of deaths "would seem too trivial" (Bhakdi, *Corona False Alarm* s.d.) to spark the desired state of social panic.

Maybe those German "experts" at the March 2020 meeting were right to doubt the insufficiently shocking impact of Covid death statistics were they to be separated out from the verbal and symbolic fog of case counts. According to the CDC's latest estimate of the IFR (Infection Fatality Rate) of Covid, issued on 10 September 2020, the chance that an infected person will die (converting the ratios into percentages and dividing by age groups) are these:

0-19 years old: 0.003 percent
20-49 years old: 0.02 percent
50-69 years old: 0.5 percent
70+ years old:5.4 percent

And it should be remembered that the number of those labeled as infected is, owing to obvious limits in testing capacity, itself a fairly low percentage of the entire population of those who have probably had the virus, something that, if taken into account would make the announced IFRs even lower. And if the estimates of this US government organization do not inspire confidence, take a look at the meta-study on global IFR by John Ioannidis of Stanford, one of the most cited scientists in the world, published in the Bulletin of the World Health Organization on October 14th, 2020, which sets the global IFR at 0.23 percent.

This systematic abuse of the so-called "case" counts would not have much significance if it were not for the fact that it is the lever that governments use to justify what are, in reality, the arbitrary arrests of millions of citizens.

Sound like an exaggeration?

Not to Portuguese justices Margarida Ramos de Almeida and Ana Pamarés, from that country's Lisbon Court of Appeal. Unlike many judges, lawyers and citizens in other places who defer to government-chosen experts and their very narrow views of public health and citizen freedom, the two Portuguese justices showed themselves to be people possessing both a comprehensive vision of societal welfare and an historically-informed understanding of the fragility of democratic freedoms.

And unlike so many self-proclaimed lovers of science in government agencies and the press, they actually took the time to read it in raw form, while applying a healthy dose of skepticism to the claims made on its behalf by those same, often Pharma-controlled, experts in government agencies.

The decision responds to a petition for *habeas corpus* made by a group of four German tourists who, under the rules established by the Regional Health Authority of the Azores Islands, were ordered into quarantine because a PCR test done on one of them upon their arrival in Portugal came back positive. This, after a test taken by the same person in Germany three days before had come back negative. The reason the judges gave for upholding the plaintiffs' claims of having been victims of an illegal detention can be summarized in the following terms:

1. No edict of an administrative unit of the government can exceed or cancel the rules relating to the privation of citizen liberty found in the Constitution of the Republic.
2. No emergency or perception of emergency can override this essential power.
3. The only people qualified to make a diagnosis of a disease are licensed doctors who have made an empirical observation of the symptomatic reality of the patient. No laboratory test can replace this essential function of the physician. Any activity that seeks to replace this function is illegal.
4. PCR tests are clearly quite unreliable when it comes to accurately detecting disease. According to the judges' reading of the available science, they are wholly useless as detectors of disease when operating beyond 25 cycles of amplification. And even at this level they have a reliability of only 70 percent.

In summary, the Portuguese judges understand a) the basic principles of protecting the rights of citizens in a regime that wants to call itself democratic b) the importance of observable physical evidence in diagnosing disease, as well as c) the irreplaceable role of physicians in the creation and assignment of diagnoses.

Viewed still more broadly, we might say that they recognized the RT-PCR test for what it has become at this point in history: a kind of medical correlate to the Orwellian concept of "thought crime" that marks those testing positive as having less civic value than others, something which, in turn, allows unscrupulous and largely unelected government authorities to effectively condemn such people before they have done anything remotely criminal, or have been definitively proven to be a danger to the society.

At the beginning of the 1990s in New York, the media encouraged a panic about the supposed existence of rampant gangs of young black and Hispanic "predators" in the city. In response, Giuliani and his collaborators invented the "stop and frisk" campaign to alleviate the growing anxieties of the rich from Manhattan who formed the core of his financial and media support. The result was the *de facto* suspension of the constitutional rights of people of color in the inner city for two decades.

We are currently the objects of a propaganda campaign designed to foment panic within our lives, and in this way, detach us from our most basic democratic customs and intuitions. Seeing how easily we have given in to the elimination of these basic rights during these last eight months, do you really think that the powers will feel compelled to give them back to us any time soon?

5 December 2020

THE COVID HORRORS: A LOVE STORY

f you can take your mind off the hot-knife-through-butter destruction of basic liberties currently taking place in the name of the fight against Covid, you can actually learn interesting new things about the thought processes of your fellow human beings.

For example, most reasonably well-educated citizens of Europe and North America believe that while organized campaigns of propaganda might in fact exist, they themselves are certainly among those least susceptible to their charms.

They know this in the same way they know that all their children are beautiful and smart, and that mistaking a plutocratic pussy-grabber for a working-class champion stems from ignorance, an error of judgment that they, of course, effortlessly avoid thanks to their long years of schooling.

I recently took a dance with the Covid bug. When we hit the floor, she did step on my toes a bit, but far fewer times than that ballerina named Flu who took me out for a twirl on the hardwood last February.

When I was sure she had left the building, I told some smart friends about the experience, and added, "Since I had actually read statistics about the chances of dying from the disease, I was never really worried during the process."

Judging from the reaction, you might have thought that I had announced that I had signed up for a lifetime membership to "Pussy-Grabbers United."

I was swiftly told —despite the clear and unassailable fact that some 90+ percent of the people who get Covid (even those past the age of 70) experience it more or less as I had – that I was indeed "very lucky."

When I asked why they insisted on portraying my experience in this way, I heard, in buckshot succession, about a cousin, the nurse friend of a friend, and, of course, all the people seen in media reports who had suffered much more than me.

And all my smart friends all seemed to agree that these decontextu-alized anecdotes had much more to say about the true threat posed by the disease than my tired old set of verified statistics.

Somewhat exasperated, I finally responded:

"You regularly get on planes to fly because, on one level or another, you know it is quite statistically safe for you to do so. Imagine if, during ten months, you were treated to anecdote after anecdote about the lives lost in air crashes, complete with graphic reconstructions of the excru-ciating last moments of the ill-fated passengers. The stats wouldn't change, but I suspect new doubts would be generated in many of you about the safety of flying."

Would it be your right to change your disposition toward flying after hearing these stories?

Certainly. Would the stories be real? Yes. Would they actually change your chances of dying in an airline crash? No. Those chances would remain exactly the same.

So, then it would be your choice as to which part of your brain you were going to listen to when it came to flying. Silence. And in typical, conflict-averse bourgeois custom, a swift end to the conversation.

You see, today's smart people clearly can't be propagandized.

Rather they simply assimilate the truths that other smart and oh-so-obviously disinterested people provide them.

And after having demonstrated their passionate and enduring love for Reality™ for all to see (after all, you never want to be caught out as being insensitive or obtuse!), they muse superciliously about those poor, less intelligent souls who live mired in a world of dangerous misinformation and emotionally charged anecdotes.

3 January 2021

WAS I JUST WITNESS TO A COVID DEATH?

Friday night at 4:45 in the morning my partner K. and I awoke to the flashing lights of police and medical teams outside the place where we are currently staying. It was accompanied by murmured conversations between the uniformed people and one of the men who often boards with our landlord, who lives in an adjacent part of the same building.

Tired and not wanting to intrude on the lives of people we knew, but not intimately, we went back to sleep, hoping that nothing really transcendent had occurred.

By mid-morning those hopes were thoroughly dashed when K. returned to our place ashen-faced to tell me that Pete, our 60-year-old weight-lifting landlord, who could have passed for a robust 45, was dead, quite possibly by suicide. We just sat there numb for a very, very long time.

Over the last few months while living in the in-law apartment of his house, K., a woman who naturally invites emotional openness in others, had come to know Pete fairly well. And on my more or less extended visits to the little apartment, I had engaged with him as well.

He was extremely bright and gentle, a yacht captain by trade and a romantic adventurer by predilection, who talked longingly and wistfully of lost loves and of business deals gone bad. Speaking to his best friend, Dave, yesterday after the tragedy, we were both confirmed in our suspicion that he was, in many ways, his own worst enemy.

But a message that came across just as strongly, if not stronger, was that Pete was deeply loved and supported by a network of friends who had remained true to him, and they to him, over a half a century. As Dave explained they had all seen each other through difficult moments, ratifying their support for each other, at times through, among other things, the lending of not insignificant sums of money.

Indeed, as we spoke, just around the corner in the gorgeous, if decadently unkempt, tropical backyard of the house with its irregularly-shaped pool, the members of that support crew were sitting together drinking beer while crying and laughing about their friend. This once grand property had, in effect, been their clubhouse, the place where they had reaffirmed their friendship over and over again during 50 years (Pete grew up in the house and had inherited it from his parents) with what he and they, and the women in their lives, liked to call Funday Sundays.

But over the last several months, that vital social lifeline, along with the possibilities of work in the boating industry, had been, if not wholly severed, severely weakened by the social restrictions imposed by the "fight against Covid."

Pete had fallen into a very deep depression, about which he had spoken pretty openly about with K. Last week, he told her he had finally gone to a mental health professional for help. But last Friday night, it seems, he decided to end things.

That said, I nonetheless feel compelled to ask all those out there currently justifying draconian reductions of basic human liberties, and worse yet, human customs of love and caring, on the basis of inflated "case" numbers spawned by a deeply flawed PCR test, as well as a 0.23 percent IFR, if they might be willing to admit that Pete was also a real Covid fatality.

And more fundamentally, I'd like to ask all those that constantly tell us about the grave threat posed by Covid—with its 99.77 percent survival rate and victim cohort tilted overwhelmingly to those at or beyond their normal level of life expectancy—if, after playing profligately and abusively with the threat of death, they have any empathy left for the very real and concrete terminations of life, catalyzed, if not caused, by their serial exaggerations.

Or do they simply consider such questions to be another thing to be "deplatformed," along with all of the other stories that don't neatly affirm the media's dominant narrative?

12 January 2021

HYSTERIA IS A FORCE THAT
GIVES US MEANING

Sadly, for most people today, World War I, or what some older Brits still refer to as the Great War, doesn't mean too much. This is too bad as it is perhaps the best mirror we have on the behavior of people and countries during the Covid era.

For those who have forgotten, WWI occurred at a time when technological advances enabled a sudden quantum leap in man's ability to slaughter his fellow man. And armed with these new killing powers, people proceeded to go out and do precisely that in absolutely staggering numbers, and on the most flimsy of nationalist pretexts.

But, believe it or not, this heretofore unthinkable level of calculated murder is not even the most instructive element of this history for us today.

Rather, it is the fact that, at the time, most people not only bought into these flimsy pretexts, but that they did so with an astonishingly high degree of zeal and enthusiasm.

The officer-butchers standing in the trenches sending wave after wave of innocent boys "over the top" – boys who could in many cases not even speak the official language of the country they were fighting for– were consistently portrayed as wise men and heroes in the press when they were, in fact, as mad as the proverbial hatter.

Under the influence of what we can now see was the first great wave of mass propaganda, the young cannon fodder proudly marched off to war convinced they were doing something important and valuable for their families and communities, when in fact they were just being sacrificed like farm animals for the delusions of men wearing epaulets or seeking to secure election victories.

It was mass stupidity in a way humanity had never seen it . . . and embraced by nearly all on the home front out of the fear of not wanting to be ostracized by their neighbors.

And when it was over, and millions had perished, or been displaced and disfigured, none of the architects of this unprecedented human disaster was ever really held to account.

For the most part, citizens continued to accept the notion that military wise men were, in fact, wise, and that the government leaders who had whipped everyone up into a mortal frenzy were still basically worth listening to and following.

Though the remaining sparks of our Enlightenment mindset often inhibit us from thinking frankly along these lines, the fact is herd stupidity and group hysteria are among the most powerful and enduring human traits.

The big mistake of so-called rational thinking is consistently underestimating the power of people's need to believe in something transcendent of what they, at one point or another in their life, come to realize is their own cosmic insignificance.

Some fill this existential lack by building loving and creative relationships with those around them. But many others, struggling under the cruel burdens imposed by often predatory consumer capitalism, find they are unable to do so.

Instead, they seek to fill this spiritual gap with the self-interested myths of togetherness provided by the cynical elites and gaily walk off the cliffs before them convinced that by doing so, they will finally bring an end to that nagging empty feeling inside.

Or, to paraphrase the title of the wonderful book by Chris Hedges on the perverse attractions of war, "Hysteria is a Force that Gives us Meaning".

30 January 2021

THE RIGHTS OF THE NATURALLY IMMUNE

There is an important issue that, in the midst of all the talk of vaccines, has not gotten nearly the attention it deserves: the civil rights of those who have already developed natural immunity to SARS-CoV-2, the virus that is said to cause Covid.

Yesterday, I got the results of the test I took to detect whether I had developed a T-Cell response to the virus.

Like the antibody test I took almost 2 months ago, it was positive.

These two things would appear to demonstrate that for all intents and purposes my body knew exactly what to do with this virus and that it probably has the equipment to dispose of it again were it, or one of its cousins, to revisit me in the near-to-medium term.

And even if one or another related strain were to visit me in that future, studies suggest strongly that the attack would be considerably less virulent than the one I overcame without excessive trouble in December.

In a halfway rational world, what to do going forward in regard to getting a vaccine for the SARS-CoV-2 virus would be something I'd discuss with my doctor in the discreet quarters of the examination room. Were it to be offered, I would politely refuse it. And he, seeing the test evidence in my file, would raise no objection.

And since the danger to me in the future from the virus is minuscule, and the science has clearly borne out what Fauci and Maria Van Kerkhove of the WHO flatly said was true before someone upstairs got to them— that asymptomatic transmission of respiratory diseases of this type is virtually nonexistent—I'd be free to live my life as I pleased without a mask, and with complete freedom of movement.

But instead of this, I am facing enormous pressure to get a vaccine in order to recover my basic rights as a citizen. And even then, those in charge are saying, I will still have to run around with a completely useless, breath-robbing and personality-canceling mask on my face.

And all this for a disease that, even before the introduction of vaccines, gave those infected by it a roughly 997.7 out of 1,000 chance of survival.

The civil authorities have decided, in effect, that fully indemnified pharmaceutical companies, whose pasts are obscenely littered with fraud, and the calculated creation of crises in order to up revenues on their products (OxyContin anyone?), have the *de facto* "right" to force me to take an experimental vaccine that, in the very, very best of circumstances, will only match what my apparently well-functioning body has already given me without any side effects.

And this, while straight out telling me that even if I submit to their government-coerced medical experiment I will probably still not get my full constitutional rights back.

This is an important issue that needs to be addressed much more vigorously than has been the case up until now.

9 March 2021

YOU ARE DAMAGED AND ONLY
WE CAN REPAIR YOU

In the gray sky under muted stars,
Flapping their wings in the silent night
Come the flocks with hairy feet
To suck the fresh blood of the herd

They eat it all
They eat it all
They eat it all,

And leave nothing behind

"The Vampires" by José "Zeca" Afonso,
Portuguese singer anti-Salazar dissident (1963)

Fifteen years ago, a good Uruguayan friend said to me, "Tom, we are at the end of an era, not just any historical period, but an era. I don't know what will come next, but I'm sure that almost all the structures that regulate our world today are no longer valid."

Although I was well into the process of radically questioning the fantasies pumped out daily in my country about the culminating time-lessness of the rules-based order erected by the United States at the end of World War II, the flat, confident tone of my friend from down under still managed to disturb me.

And it set in motion a very long series of reflections about the enormous blindness that people, even so-called thinking people, who live and work at the heart of the world system of economic power and cultural production, often suffer.

It has been stated on more than one occasion that the modern novel, defined more than anything else by its extraordinary diversity of voices, and the constant dialogue between them, was born with the publication of Cervantes' *Don Quixote*.

And within this same critical framework, many have seen its protagonist's famous shout of "I know who I am" as a statement of principles for the emergence of modern man, a being who, in contrast to his medieval predecessor, placed much greater value on his own perceptions of reality, and demonstrated an increased confidence in his own ability to successfully navigate the multiple contingencies of life.

It was not so much that the role played by God in the previous age was excluded from the mental framework of the new modern man. It was rather that man appropriated a much larger parcel of the responsibilities and privileges that social pedagogies had previously said belonged exclusively to God and his small group of anointed representatives on earth.

We can say that, in a sense, modern man or, perhaps more accurately, the small educated class that adhered to the new principles of modernity, began the process that continues to this day of progressively deifying themselves while systematically ignoring and denigrating the accumulated wisdom of those who could not, or did not want to share in the new vision of reality.

The first sustained dissent against this radical change of criteria within the bourgeois class came from the romantics of central Europe in the early 19th century, followed at the turn to the next century by thinkers such as Nietzsche, Bergson and Ortega who, each in his own way, warned about the very harmful secondary effects of the process, at first sight so laudable, of separating man from his most primary instincts and customs.

The vigorous resurrection of Western culture (1945-1975) after its two clear attempts at self-immolation (1914-1918 and 1939-1945) seemed to invalidate the pessimistic views of these earlier thinkers.

Or perhaps not.

As Pasolini tried to convince us in the 1960s, and even more fervently in the early 1970s before his death, possibly at the hands of the Italian Deep State, we should not and cannot place our faith in cultural recovery based on the propagation of consumerism.

This, for a very simple reason: consumerism, with its absolute contempt for the past, is nothing more and nothing less than an anti-culture, a force that devours everything, including the idea, so essential for the growth and maintenance of modernity, of the willful person disposed to challenge the orthodoxies propagated by the great centers of political and social power.

If there is a master trope in the discourse of consumerism, it is this: "You are defective and we, only we, can repair you." Listening to this in advertising on a day-to-day basis, works, in time, and in the effective absence of any other attractive model of the good life, like the waves that wear down the sharp edges the stones located near the tide line at the beach.

Looking at our Covidophobic, or perhaps more accurately, Covidophilic world of 2021, it seems clearer and clearer that the long agony of modernity may finally be at its end.

Westerners are very tired, so tired that they are not even interested in minimally investigating the very questionable pronouncements of the oracles of the new church of biosafety.

The signs of what Unamuno called "the reason of unreason" are everywhere.

Like the peasants of yesteryear with their garlic necklaces, people now devotedly wear masks that, no matter what the public health authorities and their media lackeys say and repeat, have no clear-cut, scientifically proven efficacy against the transmission of the virus.

And they cannot wait to take an experimental and a not fully licensed vaccine for a disease that has an overall survival rate of more than 99.7 percent.

And they accept as unquestionably legitimate methods for the containment of the virus, freedom-robbing lockdowns that, when studied rigorously in a comparative framework, show no clear sign of having positively affected infection curves or death rates in the places where they have been employed.

In effect, consumerism has done what none of the reactionary movements of the past or the many self-inflicted wounds of the

Enlightenment were able to do: empty the modern being of his desire to manage life along rational lines in the expectation of ever greater freedoms.

After sixty years of being bombarded by images designed to make us constantly doubt the often miraculous self-sufficiency of our bodies and our individual powers of discernment, we have surrendered to the law of "experts" paid by, and loyal to, big business.

Returning to Cervantes, it could be said that we no longer "know who we are" and it seems that, for most people, this loss of will and prerogative is not the slightly bit problematic.

Why worry?

Why look at the previously essential question of how to manage both risk and our own libidinal forces, they say, when we have well-credentialed sages, working hand-in-glove with power who, like the princes of the church in days past, clearly know so much more about our defective lives than do we ourselves.

2 April 2021

THE SECULARIZATION OF ORIGINAL SIN

When the concept of original sin is mentioned today, it is done, more often than not in the somewhat arcane realms of theological disputes and theological history. And given the now largely secular nature of most Western societies, this is understandable, and probably fitting.

However, this highly delimited contemporary treatment of the concept—one by the way that I find very interesting and fruitful to contemplate on the personal level—can also blind us to its enormous and highly consequential social role as an enabler of hierarchical and largely authoritarian organizational practices during the course of many centuries.

To be born "fallen," as the saying goes, is to be marked by an irremediable fragility which, in turn, impels one inexorably toward the arms of others in search of the succor we both need and want. It may even impel us, in time, to create fairly complex organizations devoted to safeguarding the common good of those who voluntarily subscribe to them.

So far, so good.

What history shows us is not so good, however, is when a group of elites establishes itself the prime if not sole arbiter of the processes in which the individual must participate if he or she is to have any hope of transcending their allegedly fallen state. In this context, original sin, which is to say the belief in the core insufficiency of the individual before god and others, becomes little more than an open justification for a never-ending series of rituals designed to reinforce the supplicatory posture of the many before power and prerogatives of those few making and reinforcing the rules.

This, in grossly simplified terms, is what the Church of Rome did, or at least sought to do, for roughly 1,500 years, before secular modernity, building upon the incremental critiques of Church-managed schemes of redemption implicit in the Renaissance, and expressed more openly the Reformation, convinced many, if not most of their inherent worthiness and resilience before the world.

It is, I think, never a waste of time to try and put ourselves in the place of others and to imagine how they see the world. If for example, I were part of a small group of people made fabulously wealthy and powerful by the existing social order, and I saw clear signs of that order's demise on the horizon—a demise seemingly caused by a rapidly growing skepticism in many quarters regarding the guiding mythologies of its operations—how might I respond?

It is nice to think that I would look inward and ask myself what I and my fellow oligarchs had done to lose the trust of the people, to make them so increasingly boisterous and irreverent in the face of what were once our largely unquestioned mandates regarding their behavior?

History, however, shows us the powerful seldom react in this manner. Most, such as, for example, the Count-Duke Olivares in mid-17th century Spain and Anthony Blinken today, simply, and ultimately quite futilely, double down on the methods they have used previously.

However, others of a more cerebral cast blessed with an understanding of Havel's maxim that "consciousness precedes being" might set out to radically re-engineer the cognitive parameters of—to use Benedict Anderson's felicitous phrase—the "Imagined Community" they and their fellow elites had done so much to create and maintain.

How to do so? How to re-engineer what the cultural theorist Even-Zohar calls "proneness" in populations that have become increasingly alienated from the key philosophical precepts and reward systems over which you and your powerful friends preside?

The obvious answer, it would seem, is to engineer a new and acute sense of fragility within people who until very recently, had more or less viewed themselves in terms of modernity's paradigms of individual liberty, autonomy, will-driven behavior...and then to use your effective control of society's key media centers to subtly redefine longstanding practices in a way that puts the individual in a defensive and ultimately supplicatory posture before the centers of power you and you small group of allies control.

For example, during the last 21 months we have all become habituated to talking about Covid-19 "cases," and seeing them as indicators *per se* of considerable individual and/or group threats to our well-being.

Left largely unexamined in all this is the fact that most of the "cases" we are referring to are not cases at all according to the long-standing canons of modern medicine wherein such determinations have always been driven by disease symptomatology as confirmed by a licensed practitioner.

Now, all of a sudden the results from a notoriously flawed and experimental RT-PCR test (remember it is being deployed on an Experimental Use Authorization) which almost across the board is run at Ct levels known by all the authorities in positions of policy-making power, including Fauci himself, to produce abundant false positives, were being treated by our media, and in time, sadly, by most of us, as confirmed health problems, subject to draconian restrictions on personal liberties.

That no symptomatology was present in the vast majority of the cases and the fact that no doctor had ever confirmed the existence of sickness all of a sudden did not matter.

These perfectly healthy people were now considered "fallen" in the health sense, and basically told the only way they could be redeemed; that is, permitted to recover their full constitutional rights, was to follow a course of "rehabilitation" capriciously determined by the authorities and enforced by legal sanction.

Could the desire to invert the core premises of modern democracy—that people are delivered to the world in a more or less existentially sufficient state and that freedom is an inherent right and not a privilege—through the strategic issuance of stigmas, be made any clearer?

Fundamental to further facilitating this civic backfooting of large swathes of the population was the fiction of frequent asymptomatic spread from SARS-type viruses. As both Anthony Fauci and Maria Van Kerkhove of the WHO sustained in no uncertain terms before someone apparently convinced them to change their stories, asymptomatic transmission with viruses like SARS-CV2 is exceedingly rare.

But why publicize this largely incontrovertible scientific fact—one clearly borne out in, among other studies, the massive Chinese investigation on the matter published in November, 2020 —when you can have the specter of ever-present infection; that is, the specter of personal fallenness hanging over much of the society?

This fable of massive asymptomatic transmission was, and is, especially useful in ensuring that the young buy into the emergent paradigm of civic freedom not as an inalienable right but as a privilege bestowed conditionally by technocratic elites.

Though the media sought from the first moment to falsely portray Covid-19 as an age-indifferent threat, even the most obtuse believer in mainstream media fallacies could not help but notice that its toll of severe illness and death was overwhelmingly tilted toward the elderly.

The answer to this "problem," one eerily mapped out in the so-called "Panic paper" leaked from secret German government deliberations at the outset of the epidemic, was to instill in children the idea that, owing to the alleged phenomenon of asymptomatic transmission, their continued embrace of normal freedoms unconditioned by outside regimes of control could lead to the deaths of those people they most love and need.

This same emotional blackmail rooted in a scientific fiction—and moreover one known to the highest authorities from the outset as such— was the driver behind the absurd school closure policies pursued in this country and abroad during the last year. This, despite the fact that studies on in-school transmission from several European countries had debunked it as early as May 2020.

From the point of view of economic and government elites concerned about losing their entrenched prerogatives, nothing is more threatening than the creation of voluntary webs of solidarity among the population.

And historically, schools have played an absolutely crucial role in this process. Indeed, they are generally the first places where we discover ideas and concepts other than those we learned at the dinner table or in houses of worship, and learn to overcome the frictions these clashes of ideas can create through measured dialogue. In short, schools are the places we take our first steps toward becoming political beings.

When viewed in this light, could there be anything better for these same elites than having children trapped at home in front of a screen plying them with well-engineered "behavioral nudges" instead on the playground discovering the different ways of thinking of their friends and acquaintances, and developing ways to form bonds of social solidarity that might eventually allow them to challenge entrenched centers of power?

Could there be anything more beneficial to securing this necessary state of alienation than to train students to see their perfectly harmless fellow classmates as perpetually dangerous vectors of infection, so dangerous to others that their faces, whose expression we know to be absolutely essential to the development of bonds of empathy and social intelligence in the young, must be covered up?

All of which brings us finally to the matter of Covid-19 and naturally acquired immunity.

One of the basics of modern marketing, like those original-sin-rooted systems of social control in the past, is to constantly remind people of their core insufficiency before basic life challenges. Though it takes numerous verbal and semiotic forms, the mantra "You are broken, and we are here to fix you" lies at the core of many, if not most campaigns of consumer persuasion.

Over the last several decades, drug companies, hungry for the creation of new profit centers in a largely saturated market (from the point of view of products necessary for basic survival and the extension of life) have recurred assiduously to this basic trope.

Indeed, they have used the advertising largesse afforded them by their enormous profit margins to speak directly to the consumer about his or her real or imagined frailties. They also use this financial power to silence corporate journalists from looking into the veracity of these claims of human insufficiency by threatening to deprive their parent companies of their massive ad-buys should the investigative journalists go too far in their research.

Over the las 21 months, one of the more constant messages we have received from the press is the SARS-CoV-2 is a wholly "novel" virus about which very little is known and that therefore we must proceed in the most cautious and risk-averse ways possible, starting, in effect, from ground zero in the matter of scientific assumptions.

However, for numerous scientists of consolidated prestige this is patently absurd. They know that members of their profession have been studying Coronaviruses for several decades now, and that they understand a great deal about each strain, as well as the many traits and behaviors they have in common. This fact is eloquently borne out by the fact that Corman and Drosten, the German scientists whose hastily approved paper established the protocol for RT-PCR testing methods currently being used to detect SARS-CoV-2 infections across the world relied, not on the existence of genetic material from that particular "novel" virus when plotting the test, but rather a 2003 SARS-CoV virus owing, as they candidly admit, to "the close genetic relatedness" of the two viruses.

Scientists have also long-known about the human body's extraordinary ability to develop robust and lasting cross-immunity through antibody and T-Cell responses to numerous variants of a given coronavirus, an agility that very few if any of the newly developed experimental vaccines have, or seemingly expect to have.

In fact, after managing to keep these basic facts out of the mainstream press through the ""We-just-don't-know-enough-about-this-completely-new-virus" and "The-matter-of-reinfection-is-still-very-unclear" bluffs, the proof of these long-understood immunological potencies are emerging in the scientific literature on SARS-CoV-2.

If authorities and their servants in the press were, in fact, interested in getting this country and others back on their feet as soon as possible, this news, or perhaps I should say this long-known reality, like the fact that for anyone under 65 the chances of dying from Covid-19 are truly miniscule, and for children and young adults virtually nil, would be widely trumpeted.

Instead those that bring forth these facts, like Martin Kulldorff when he uttered the self-evident truth that "there is no need to vaccinate everyone" find themselves increasingly banned from expressing their views in social media.

Making this blatant suppression of the good news of natural immunity even more irritating and frankly alarming, is the dubious suggestion from our health agencies that the experimental vaccines confer greater breadth and duration of immunity, and protection against transmission, than does natural immunity.

As the applications for Emergency Use Authorizations for these vaccines make quite clear, and subsequent data has confirmed in spades, none of the manufacturers claim in any forthright way that these vaccines will either protect those that take them from getting infected, or passing the virus on to others. The only claims they make are in the realm of lessening the severity of effects of those who do become infected.

Finally, there is the matter of the unknown effects of not fully tested vaccines. Strong warnings about the possible very negative health effects of vaccinating those who have had Covid-19 with mRNA vaccines have been issued by among many others, Drs.Peter McCullough, Hooman Norchashm, and Patrick Whelan.

Thinking about it, one cannot help but note the absurd double standard at play when it comes to the application of the precautionary principle with Covid.

In our present reality, the precautionary principle can *always* be invoked to curtail human freedoms even though the threat is, as we have seen, demonstrably small and the techniques that are said to be serving in the cause of prevention (masks and lockdowns) have absolutely no robust science backing their efficacy.

But it is almost *never* invoked when it comes to not fully tested vaccines, injections manifestly not needed by the vast majority of the population, and produced by profit-driven companies who have arranged for complete immunity from damages produced by their products!

When we look dispassionately at the way the Covid-19 phenomenon has been handled, it is clear we are not so much up against a massive biological threat to human survival, but rather a concerted culture-planning effort on the part of monied and governmental elites across the Euro-American world, and quite possibly beyond, to dispense with the core premise of democratic governance in the contemporary era—that governments work for the people and not vice-versa—and replace it with a relationship of dependence in which technocratic elites, like the priests and archbishops of the Medieval church who worked in concert with the lords of the manor to exercise effective control over most, if not all aspects of the life of the individual.

And if all this sounds like tinfoil talk, then I would remind you of the response that the great scholar of "Deep Politics" Michael Parenti customarily gives when people accuse him of being a so-called "conspiracy theorist:"

"The alternative is to believe that the powerful and the privileged are somnambulists, who move about oblivious to questions of power and privilege; that they always tell us the truth and have nothing to hide even when they hide so much; that although most of us ordinary people might consciously try to pursue our own interests, wealthy elites do not; that when those at the top employ force and violence around the world it is only for the laudable reasons they profess; that when they arm, train, and finance covert actions in numerous countries, and then fail to acknowledge their role in such deeds, it is because of oversight or forgetfulness or perhaps modesty; and that it is merely a coincidence how the policies of the national security state so consistently serve the interests of the transnational corporations and the capital-accumulation system throughout the world."

I understand the psychological reflex that leads many, if not most, people to ascribe essentially benign motives to those to whom we have bequeathed disproportionately large parcels of financial and political power, and the implicit right to frame transversally accepted notions of social "truth." It is the same reflex that impedes most of us from entertaining the fact that our parents might be vicious and amoral businesspeople, or worse yet, pedophiles and murderers.

But the fact is that there are a small number of parents who act precisely in these ways, and pretending that this is not or cannot be so will do nothing to stop them from hurting other people. Life is intrinsically beautiful. But if we really want to safeguard that beauty and pass it on to our children and grandchildren, we must be prepared, as mature adults, to see and confront authoritarian campaigns of coercion and social control when they stare us in the face.

12 April 2021

AN INTERVIEW WITH A VERY DANGEROUS MAN[2]

Editor's Note: *Upon reading the last piece by our columnist TH, in which he again questions key elements of the Covid narrative, a valued member of our subscription community dubbed him a "very dangerous man" and, backed by others, called for his firing from the paper. Concerned about his well-being we sent our crack correspondent Thomas Harrington out to talk with him. The text below is the record of their conversation.*

Thomas Harrington: Where are you right now?

Very Dangerous Man: For reasons of operational security, I don't usually talk publicly about my location. Let's just say that I am in a safe place from whence I can plan more extremely dangerous essayistic attacks on the well-being of the citizens of Catalonia.

TH: What is a typical day in the life of a Very Dangerous Man like you?

VDM: I think Hollywood has given us too glamorous a view of Very Dangerous Men like me. The truth is that my days are pretty boring. I read a lot and sometimes I write. I also work in my capacity as a teacher

---

2 Between October of 2019 and February 2022 I had a monthly column at the small but influential Catalan daily *Vilaweb*. During that time, I emerged, for better or worse, as one the more harsh and constant critics in the Catalan press of the both Catalan and Spanish government approaches to containing the virus. The essay you see here is an English translation of a column I published in June of 2021 in that paper. N.B. the editor in the Editor's note is not the real editor of the paper, but a figment of my literary imagination. The rest of the piece, however, is solidly anchored in reality.

to corrupt the minds of my students, asking them incisive questions and demanding they bolster their arguments, not on the basis of "People say," "I have heard" and "Everyone knows," but with documented studies discovered as part of their own research.

TH: Did you always aspire to be a Very Dangerous Man?

VDM: VDM: Yes. I realized this for the first time at the age of two when my grandfather asked me what I wanted to be when I grew up. And without thinking twice I told him (I remember it like it was yesterday!) I wanted to be "a Very Dangerous Man." But over the years, I discovered that doing so was much harder than saying it. In those years you usually had to do something very big like sell nuclear secrets to the official enemy of the moment, or like Ellsberg, steal the documents that showed that the US government knew from the early 1960s that the war in Vietnam was an exercise in futility and that, therefore, the deaths of millions of Vietnamese, and about 60,000 American soldiers were completely unnecessary. That's how things were until recently.

But now everything has changed.

Now the barriers to entry for those wanting to enter the previously small circle of VDMs have been dramatically lowered. Now it's enough to simply use an incorrect pronoun, or state that no matter how much you don't agree, even remotely, with everything that their leaders do, countries like Russia, Syria or China also have legitimate national and territorial interests.

But the fastest and surest way to achieve ascension to the VDM circle is to cite scientific studies that suggest that "The Science"™ quoted by the press, and the scientists chosen by the ruling class to explain Covid to the masses—leaders, doctors and epidemiologists who, of course, never receive or give in to the pressures of the great centers of international economic power or think to use crises to increase their control over the public—might not be telling us everything we need to know in order to respond in the most democratically responsible way to the challenge of Covid. It works every time.

TH: Are you suggesting that science is based, above all, on the rigorous and constant debate and confrontation of various explanations of reality? ...And what's more, that there may be people and entities, that for their own interests, may have a desire to restrict the parameters of the debates on the best way to fight the virus?

What you are saying is outrageous!!

Pardon the digression, but I would like to add a little context for our sensitive and impressionable readers out there reminding them of the fact that while everything the press said before November of 2016 was absolutely true, we are now in the perilous new era of fake news and that they should keep this in mind as they listen to the words of this Very Dangerous Man. They should also remember that drug companies are love-fueled charities that think of nothing but improving the human condition 24 hours a day and would never think of, say, encouraging opioid addiction among the US population for years, or promoting drugs of marginal utility but recommended lifelong use to increase their own income. And that these companies will ever use the enormous amounts of money they earn to influence the media and civic processes of the societies in which they operate.

It's like suggesting, for example that the prime minister of Spain would change the Spanish constitution on a summer afternoon in 2011 to please the big European banks, or that Prime Minister Pedro Sánchez, attentive to the wishes of the Deep State powers in Madrid, has no interest in entering into serious negotiations about the political status of Catalonia within Spain. In other words, we must always be attentive to the fog of misinformation around us and those that spread it like the subject of this interview.

VDM: I appreciate your digression as it gives me more opportunities to strengthen my credentials as a VDM before the public. I would not only like to reaffirm the idea that free debate is absolutely central to all scientific and governmental processes, but add that censorship in the so-called democratic countries has reached levels not seen in 70 years if not more, and that the parameters of the debate on policies relating to Covid within the Spanish state are among the narrowest in the Western world.

It is not clear why this is so. But I think we can find some clues in the work of the great scholar of propaganda, Jacques Ellul, who suggested that the bourgeois class is always the prime center of support for the propaganda codes devised by the super-elites to justify their "natural" control of society, imbuing this top-down propaganda with a level of a conviction that the magnates themselves lack.

Spain is a society full of relative newcomers to the bourgeois world. It is thus only understandable that in their desire to demonstrate their bourgeois *bona fides* these newly elevated citizens might bend over backwards to show their devotion to the prime mythologies of contemporary bourgeois life which, of course, include an absolute faith in modern medicine and its pharmaceutical solutions. Nor can we discount the long-term effects on a society of the experience—still largely unacknowledged—of living for almost four decades under state propaganda that constantly and subtly reminds them of the perils of a possible new Civil War, and thus of the danger of going against predominant social values. Under such circumstances fear and submission to authority become an almost natural reflex. Of course, suggesting this also makes me dangerous because it challenges the still widespread idea that both Spaniards and Catalans experienced complete cultural makeovers in the years and decades following Franco's death in 1975.

TH: What else makes you a dangerous man?

VDM: Many things. One of the most dangerous things I do is to suggest that an epidemic is a problem of a deeply interdisciplinary nature and that, therefore, the last people who should be leading an effort to combat it are doctors in general, and virologists in particular. Due to their training under the very narrow Western paradigm of the doctor as "disease hunter," they are often completely unable to contemplate the cost in other very important social goods of their much-cherished "wars" of eradication against particular diseases. They should obviously be an important part of policy discussions. But just one voice among many others. The final decisions must always be in the hands of others, preferably elected politicians, with a broader vision of the idea of public health. And if these politicians instead choose to hide behind the afore-mentioned monomaniacal "experts," we must demand they bring other civic voices to the conversation.

I am also dangerous because I suggest that a well-educated person without a scientific background (especially if he is a professional researcher used to handling large amounts of information) is generally able to read scientific literature and use what he reads to create a critical vision of the Covid problem as a whole. Moreover, I will say that those who have the time and this particular intellectual training and do not do so—thus leaving the task of creating visions of the reality of the problem in the hands of journalists and fact-checkers enslaved by the frantic pace of their work and subjected to very strong corporatist pressures—are close to negligent.

At the same time, it is important to emphasize what I am not saying: that the reading of scientific articles by non-specialists can be done with the same acuity and attention to details that specialists in the discipline could bring to the task. To state something like that would be absurd. But this does not mean that the interpretations of non-specialists are useless, or as some suggest, a kind of desecration of the cult of scientists.

If that's the case, then why are the interpretations of mainstream journalists writing and commenting on the same studies considered licit? Efforts to analyze discrete elements of a disease must always exist in a yin-yang dynamic with efforts to synthesize a view of the social problem as a whole. And most decently educated people are more than capable of doing this. All it takes is a mind dedicated to active and rigorous discernment of the complexity of life.

I am also dangerous for saying things like "criticizing the ways some are using to combat Covid is not the same as denying the existence of the virus, nor the serious problems it has caused." Or that "expressing some uneasiness about the desire of governments to vaccinate all indi-viduals in their societies with experimental vaccines that have not gone through a full cycle of safety tests for a disease that, according to the latest meta-study by John Ioannidis leaves 99.85 percent of those infected alive, is not the same as being opposed to all vaccines." Obviously inflammatory stuff.

My only purpose in saying things like this is, as everyone knows, to provoke good altruistic people, and to give vent to my only slightly hidden desire to see the maximum number of people—especially grannies—die, while at the same time giving to succor Vox and all the other fascists and proto-fascists in Spain and around the world

But the thing that makes me most dangerous is the way I torment the devotees of *Our Lady of Masks and Lockdown* and other hallowed members of the church of "The Science"™ with—get this—true scientific (that's lower case) studies, or probing questions based on scientific studies (again with a lower case) that call into question essential elements of their faith. It drives them perfectly nuts.

TH: For example?

VDM: If according to the CDC the chance of a person under 50 infected with SARS-CoV-2 (a probable small minority of the total population to begin with) dying from Covid is 0.05 percent, what reason is there for all these people to urgently take an experimental vaccine that has it not undergone the full safety testing? This, when the EUA briefing reports for the three currently available vaccines all say (Moderna (p.49), Pfizer (p.47) and Jansson (p.57) there is no evidence to prove that these injections limit the transmission of the virus?

Or an this analysis of the probable capabilities and safety profiles of the vaccines, produced by a group of 30 prestigious scientists from around the world, has not yet made its way into the mainstream press?

Or asking what exactly was the new science that led the CDC, WHO and Germany's RKI to simultaneously alter their previous highly skeptical positions on effectiveness of masks as barriers against infection in the general public?

Or, if as a recent publication suggests, there are there are serious questions about both the origin and reliability of the Corman-Drosten RT-PCR testing protocol, why isn't this being openly debated in the press?

Or why, if there is an apparent scientific consensus regarding the unreliability (in favor of false positives) of all PCR tests operated beyond

30-33 ct (Cycle thresholds), why is the FDA along with most European regulatory institutions recommending that they be run at 40 ct and up?

Or why did the CDC adopt, apparently illegally, an entirely new and completely *sui generis* protocol for counting "Covid deaths" in the spring of 2020?

And why did the authorities, who as we saw above actively promoted the appearance of "cases" by putting the recommended level of PCR testing at 40ct, suddenly just adjust it to 28ct for the purposes of calculating the number of cases now suddenly appearing in the cohort of the fully vaccinated?

Or I could ask, for example, how it is that the number of deaths per million in that terrible and irresponsible country called Sweden, where there were no generalized lockdowns and no mandatory masking, are less than in Spain with its rather strict confinement regime? Or about the fact that in the US many states without lockdowns and without mandatory public masking (e.g. Florida, Georgia, and now Texas) have the same or better results in cases and deaths than several states (California, New York, New Jersey, Massachusetts) with much stricter "mitigation" regimes?

You see, silly but apparently quite irritating stuff, with obviously no connection to the important tasks of rigorously measuring the magnitude of the problem we face and generating appropriate ways to respond to it.

Shall I continue?

TH: No. I have already heard more than enough. I now understand why you are considered a Very Dangerous Man. It seems to me that the responsible thing to be done at this point is ban you from all of the world's media platforms.

28 May 2021

THE CONSCIOUS CULTIVATION
OF IGNORANCE

The human brain has a tendency to impose binary cognitive schemas upon the sometimes unfathomable complexity of the world around us.

For example, numerous scholars of nationalism have suggested that it is often quite difficult to build a strong and durable national project in the absence of a threatening "other" whose supposed cultural inferiority and innate aggression is said to imperil the integrity of the "home" collective.

It is thus no accident, as the anthropologists Jonas Frykman and Orvar Löfgren have shown in the particular case of contemporary Sweden, that campaigns of individual and collective hygiene were often important elements of many nationalist movements of the late 19th and early 20th centuries.

Although we don't often talk about it, we also find this mental apartheid, rooted in a desire to separate the "clean" from the "dirty" in our intellectual world.

Since the Enlightenment, knowledge has been defined in terms of its relationship to ignorance; that is, against the supposedly dark wilderness of facts that are untouched by the organizing magic of well-instructed human minds and are thus considered basically useless.

Under the influence of this world view, which defines ignorance in essentially negative terms—as phenomena devoid of the allegedly inherent order of civilization—the act of removing certain cultural repertoires from the eyes of citizens becomes not just an option, but an obligation. And hence the widespread institutional pressure *not to analyze* the cultural phenomena that someone—usually from a position of power—has labeled as the product of a disordered mind.

But what if things aren't that simple?

What if it turns out that the creation of ignorance is as basic and constant a part of life as the production of knowledge, and that, moreover, the processes that generate it have readily identifiable structures and patterns? If so, might we not need to study it more closely?

This is the proposal of a growing group of researchers in a field that one of the members, the anthropologist Robert Proctor, calls 'agnotology,' and what others simply call "the study of ignorance."

The new field has many thematic thrusts. For me, the most interesting of these, one addressed by Proctor himself, is how very politically and economically powerful groups quite consciously fabricate ignorance among the population, and that they often do so—as he demonstrates effectively in his detailed study of behavior of the American tobacco industry—under the rubric of science and the need to protect people from the influence of misinformation.

None of this, of course, would surprise a veteran intelligence agent in any major country in the world, or a senior executive in a multinational company. Nor would it surprise the growing number of Behavioral Insight Team (BIT) members in the "democratic" governments of the world, or in Silicon Valley.

And needless to say, it certainly would not be news to the vast majority of people who have not been fortunate enough to spend years in college, and thus earn their keep doing hard and often soul-draining work.

In contrast, many, if not most of those who have entered the world of institutionalized intellectual activities seem to have an almost infinite capacity not only to be surprised by the possibility that all of this might be going on, but feel offended by the mere suggestion that certain people, usually of the same educational class as they, might actually be trying to deceive them and others in the name of scientific knowledge.

In the interest of maintaining their coveted sense of intellectual hygiene, they've gifted themselves with a set of verbal and thus cognitive tools such as "conspiracy theorist" (developed and deployed, according to prestigious political scientist Lance Dehaven Smith, by the CIA to eliminate awkward questions about the assassination of John F. Kennedy) to facilitate their deep desire to remain ignorant of what people from other, less institutionally-favored sites of knowledge-making might be seeing and thinking.

The latest trick of the institutionalized elites in this serial game of curbing the proliferation of fresh interpretations of reality from below is to transform science, which is defined by its disdain for dogma, into a rigid canon of authoritarian prescriptions that do not admit dialogue or dissent.

An essential element of this new game is to present the views of a very small number of scientists chosen by the powerful as the embodiment of science itself, and to free these unelected mandarins from the need to ever have to justify their thoughts and actions in the context of a debate.

Fomenting Ignorance on Natural Immunity

Given the potentially large number of people affected, one of the more important elements of the Covid phenomenon is the issue of natural immunity. For nearly two years our public health officials have used the classic ignorance-inducing tools of Big Tobacco and Big Oil—"We really don't know" and "We still don't have enough information"—to avoid a public discussion on the issue.

This, as if one of the most basic laws of immunology—that overcoming a viral attack almost always produces lasting immunity—was suddenly ruled out when it came to treating a particular variant of a well-known and well-studied family of viruses.

This wall of manufactured silence prevented tens of millions of previously-infected citizens from making halfway-informed decisions about experimental vaccines in the first months of the vaccine rollout.

When, however, in the spring of 2021 Senator Ron Johnson and Senator Rand Paul, a doctor, both announced they had recovered from Covid and thus saw no need to take the vaccine, the ignorance machine switched from passive (information restriction) to active ("reality" creation) mode.

On May 19, 2021, after several doctors with impeccable credentials had publicly confirmed the scientific obviousness of what Johnson and Paul had said, the FDA—the same FDA that was then encouraging the boundless use of wildly inaccurate PCR tests marketed on an EUA to stigmatize perfectly healthy people as sick and in need of *de facto* imprisonment—suddenly issued a new statement cautioning against the use of the *fully approved* Covid antibody tests to assess a patient's level of immunity against Covid, saying:

"Currently authorized SARS-CoV-2 antibody tests have not been evaluated to assess the level of protection provided by an immune response to Covid-19 vaccination. If antibody test results are interpreted incorrectly, there is a potential risk that people may take fewer precautions against SARS-CoV-2 exposure. Taking fewer steps to protect against SARS-CoV-2 can increase their risk of SARS-CoV-2 infection and may result in the increased spread of SARS-CoV-2."

When I asked him about this statement, and the FDA commissioner's public endorsement of it back in May, surgeon and immunologist Hooman Noorchashm stated, "It's 100 percent unscientific." He then went on to further explain the matter in a post on Medium:

"As an analogy, this FDA statement against use of Covid-19 antibodies to assess immunity is so absurd, it would be like NASA putting out a public statement advising the public that we should no longer assume that the earth is round...... the current commissioner of the FDA proudly states in a Tweet that the gold-standard serological evidence of immunity to the SARS-CoV-2 (i.e., the antibody tests for Spike protein and Nucleocapsid) means nothing in 2021. No matter that this same clinical readout (i.e., antibodies against SARS-CoV-2) was used to assess the vaccine's efficacy in the clinical trials leading to EUA approval of the Covid-19 vaccines."

We've seen the same sort of gross manipulation in regard to encouraging the widespread impression among the population that by taking the vaccines one was gaining immunity from infection and losing the ability to transmit the virus to others.

Are we really supposed to believe that the authorities pushing the vaccines and publicly suggesting that they will end infection and transmission really had not read the same EUA approvals that every thinking citizen has at their disposal since the very first months of 2021?

And this is where, in light of these phenomena, it becomes incumbent on each one of us to decide how we wish to confront the problem of information management by public authorities as we go forward.

Are we going to continue to seek refuge in what I have come to term the "juvenile" posture before such realities? This appears to be the default position of the credentialed classes, and holds that the people in our governmental and regulatory bodies are basically honest brokers who, like most of us, make mistakes owing to either understandable inattention or a lack of reliable information.

Or will we begin facing up, as adults, to the stark fact that our public institutions have been captured by a minority of people who essentially view us as a headless and manipulable biomass to be nudged in ways that benefit their long-term goals and desires, and who in the pursuit of those ends have built a very sophisticated ignorance machine to insure we continue to conform to the very low expectations they have for us as intellectuals and moral beings?

I believe we must begin to study, as one carefully studies the captured spy plane of an enemy power, exactly how that ignorance machine works. Otherwise will we continue to pretend, childlike, that these highly consequential untruths that profoundly affect our lives were a natural and largely innocent byproduct of the entropic reality of life.

It is a choice each one of us will have to make, the answers to which will have far-reaching consequences on the success or failure of our collective efforts to recover the rights and freedoms stolen from us over the last two years.

2 July 2021

THE FRIGHTENED CLASS

They're all around us, especially those of us who live in relatively prosperous metropolitan neighborhoods in the US or Western Europe. Despite being—at least in material terms—among the most fortunate people who have ever walked the earth, they are very scared. And they want you to be very frightened too.

Indeed, many of them see your refusal to be as frightened as they are about life's inevitable risks as a grave problem which entitles them and their often powerful and influential fellow travelers to recur to all manner of authoritarian practices to insure that you adhere to their increasingly neurotic view of reality.

This tendency has been in full bloom lately as the people who have sat safely behind their laptops during the last 20 months have harangued and threatened those who have been out on job sites and in meatpacking plants mixing freely with others and the virus, to internalize their own obsessions.

Viewed in historical terms, it's an odd phenomenon.

For most of recorded time prosperity and education have been the gateway to a life of relative freedom from worry. But now, the people who most enjoy these benefits are, it seems, wracked with anxiety and hellbent on sharing their misery with others.

The point here is not to belittle the very real costs of anxiety in the lives of many people, nor to dismiss it as a real public health concern. Rather, it is to ask how and why it is proliferating so rapidly among those who, at least on the surface, have less reason than the vast majority of their fellow human beings to suffer from it.

There are, I think, a number of possible explanations.

One way of explaining the phenomenon is in the context of income inequality and its devastating effects on the shape and size of the upper middle class, and on those who still believe they have a realistic chance of joining its ranks.

Those who have made it into that sub-group are deeply cognizant of the unstable nature of their status in a world of corporate buyouts and rampant layoffs. And they worry that they may not be able to provide their children with the ability to retain what they see, rightly or wrongly, as the only real version of the good life.

Thus, when the people way up on top decided following September 11th to make fear the cornerstone of political mobilization in an increasingly post-political and post-communal society, they found a ready reserve of support in this anxious if also relatively prosperous cohort of the population.

And after two decades of having their already anxious inner selves massaged daily by a steady drumbeat of fear (and a diet of Trump as Hitler for dessert) both they and their children fell like ripe fruit into the hands of those that wanted to sell them on the "unprecedented" threat posed by a disease that leaves 99.75-99.85 percent off its victims wonderfully alive.

Adding another layer to this general phenomenon is the increasing isolation of our educated classes from "physicality" in both their work and their communal lives.

Until the 1990s it was virtually impossible for anyone other than the richest of the rich not to have any active or passive acquaintance with the world of physical work. Indeed, for the first three or four decades after World War II many of those who could financially afford to relieve their children of this acquaintance with physical work often did not do so, as they believed that knowing what it meant to sweat, ache, be crushingly bored and, not infrequently, humiliated during the course of the day was essential to gaining a more rounded and empathetic understanding of the human condition.

All that ended when the financialization of the economy and the rise of the internet made what Christopher Lasch presciently termed the "rebellion of the elites" a much more palpable possibility.

For example, very few of my students have ever worked during their summers in anything other than office jobs, often procured through family connections. They thus have little understanding of, and empathy for, of just how brutal and demeaning daily work can be for so many people.

This alienation from the physical can also be seen in family life. The predominant and seldom challenged edict of "Go where the money is"—a virtual religion for those seeking upward advancement in US culture—has meant that large numbers of children now grow up far away from their extended families. However, we seldom talk about the built-in costs of subscribing to this ethos.

To talk with and listen to grandparents, uncles and aunts on a regular basis and in person is very different from seeing these people in occasional choreographed holiday rituals, or from time-to-time on Zoom. In the first instance, the child is inserted into a milieu that, for better or worse, structures his understanding of how the world works and forces him to recognize his relationship to both the past, and to the stories of other individuals.

Might they decide later, for very good reasons, to break for this particular network of narratives? Of course. But when they do so they will at least carry within the idea of a stable and rooted identity as a life goal, something that my discussions with students over the last decade have led me to believe many of them no longer see as a possibility, or even a need.

The increasing distance between those working within the antiseptic confines of the information economy and those still earning their keep with their bodies has, moreover, led many of the former group into a state of enormous confusion regarding the distinction between words and deeds.

To work in academia, as I have for the last three decades, is to be surrounded by people who truly believe that the words one exchanges with others are as existentially weighty and consequential as physical assaults upon the body. This not only shows how few of them have ever been in a real brawl, but how blind they are to the fundamental role that physical violence and/or the looming threat of its use has always played in the game of coercing the many to bend to the will of the few.

And this is probably why so many of them, parroting the moralizing, if factually tenuous, talking points supplied to them by a deeply corrupt media establishment, are so nonplussed about the *real physical assaults* upon people's bodies now taking place in the name of "fighting Covid."

It is also why a disturbing number of those whom they teach truly believe that hearing someone utter a critique against an ideological construct that another person has told them was good and correct is much more problematic than forcing someone to be injected with an experimental drug under the threat of losing their livelihood.

But perhaps the most significant reason for the rise of the Frightened Class is modern consumer culture's assault upon the millenary practice of providing the young with what Joseph Campbell called "adequate mythic instruction." For Campbell myths are, above all, a means of inoculating the young against the angst of knowing we are all destined for decrepitude and death, as well as much inflicted cruelty during that march toward oblivion.

These stories, he suggests, show the young how others have confronted their fears in the past and have learned to find meaning and coherence in the apparent absurdity of their situations. They drive home the message that there is nothing approaching vital plenitude and significant psychological growth without the repeated assumption of risk and a constant engagement with fear. In short, they instill in the young the idea that they are by no means alone in their existential dilemmas.

From the point of view of consumer culture, however, a mythically-anchored person; that is, someone able to place their present struggles in a broad, coherent and historically-informed perspective, is a very troubling thing.

Why?

Because such people are much less amenable to the mostly fear-based pitches that drive the production and consumption of the often nonessential goods upon which the system depends for its continued growth and expansion. If an adolescent has heard stories that underscore the ubiquity of awkward feelings among people of his age, and how so many before them passed through these difficulties and became stronger and wiser, then he is much less likely to pine for the purchase of the "solution" to the problem proffered to him by commercial entities.

It has been said that, over time, we tend to "become what we do." It seems that after orchestrating campaign after campaign of fear on behalf of the truly powerful, the comfortable classes have come to believe their own schtick to the point where they have trouble understanding, or even tolerating, those who have always consumed their mercenarily produced fear porn with a large helping of salt.

Worse yet, these self-frightened elites seem to think they can now remedy their lack of credibility with those living outside their grim prison of angst by simply amping up the volume on the scare machine. I suspect they soon might be in for a bigger and possibly much more "physical" set of responses than they ever imagined could come their way.

19 October 2021

THE TREASON OF THE HEALERS

n 1927, the French intellectual Julien Benda published *La Trahison des Clercs* which has been translated to English as *The Betrayal* (and sometimes the *Treason*) *of the Intellectuals*. The book is a searing indictment of the role played by intellectuals from both sides of the First World War in fanning the flames of that devastating conflict which raised the threshold of man's capacity for murder and destruction to theretofore unimaginable levels.

For Benda, the great and unpardonable sin of the intellectuals in both Germany and France was to abandon the imperative to generate disinterested knowledge, and to instead lend their talents and prestige to tasks of promoting home-borne chauvinism on one hand, and the systematic denigration of the enemy's culture and citizens on the other.

The rise of the figure of the intellectual, as we understand it today, is intimately linked to two interlocking historical processes from the last third of the 19th century: the rapid secularization of society and the rise of the daily newspaper.

In effect, as citizens began to leave the church and its leaders behind, they redirected their desire for transcendence toward the daily press and its new secular "clerics." These new spiritual leaders, in turn, had to decide, as had their predecessors in ancient Israel, Greece and Rome before them, how to exercise their newfound power.

Was it their job to shore up the positive spirit of the collective in the age of the nation-state? Or was it to reveal to their parishioner-readers the stark truths of their time?

Given the enormous stakes in the matter, the second option was, for Benda, the only morally acceptable one.

As the 20th century advanced, the turn-of-the-century writer was gradually supplanted at the apex of the new social communion by the man of science, and especially, by the figure of the physician. Given the exigencies of the scientific method, an adherence to a disinterested search for knowledge should have, if anything, become even more important for such people than it had been for the lettered objects of Benda's ire.

However, it did not take long to discover that the newly ascendant men of science were just as prone as Benda's treasonous writers to abuse the institutional powers conferred on them by society and the state in order to pursue narrowly subscribed, and often deeply inhumane, campaigns of bullying and/or human experimentation.

There was, of course the long campaign of intellectual terror waged by Lysenko and his acolytes in the Soviet Union and the large-scale buy-in—much bigger than is still generally acknowledged or admitted—by German physicians of the genocidal program of "Nazi medicine" during the 1930s and 1940s. And here at home, we have more than enough disgusting cases of medical abuse (forced lobotomies, the Tuskegee Study, MK Ultra and OxyContin to name just a few) to keep a forensic journalist or historian of medical crime busy for a lifetime.

But when it comes to acknowledging this, things are much the way they are when it comes to acknowledging the serial crimes of the US empire. It is—as Harold Pinter said in addressing this last matter in his Nobel speech—as if, "It never happened. Nothing ever happened. Even while it was happening it wasn't happening. It didn't matter. It was of no interest."

And because we have largely ignored these outrages against human dignity and the core ethos of healing—explaining them away the very few times when they are mentioned with the ever-useful "a few bad apples" meme—we find ourselves completely flat-footed before the dangers of a new expert-led imposition of highly questionable public health policies, as well as a medical cadre that is more arrogant and less capable of personal and collective insight than one could have ever believed to be possible.

Emblematic of this new reality was a dialogue about Covid containment I recently had with a doctor friend who insisted in the inimitably declamatory fashion of his caste that: "We know what we have to do to control Covid. Just use masks and social distancing."

When I expressed skepticism about this and asked him whether he, like me, had read the available science on the effectiveness of those approaches to containment, he ignored me. And when I again asked if he had read the science he said: "You can cite all the trivia you want, but we know this is what works."

Indeed, I am more and more convinced that most practicing physicians have read precious few studies on the clinical treatment of Covid or the effectiveness of the public health measures that were largeley invented out of whole cloth in March of 2020 to combat the spread of the disease.

Rather, like the hierarchically-minded "good students" they were and are, they simply assume that someone somewhere up the chain of power has actually read things about these matters, subjected them to critique, and decided they all made perfect sense. Indeed, never has Thomas Kuhn's portrayal of the stagnant, paradigm-enslaved thinking of most working scientists looked more true.

How else can we explain the fact that so many physicians have sat by silently while blatant anti-science and anti-logic nonsense is proffered to the public day after day by their media colleagues, and worse yet, have, in numerous cases, organized and led campaigns to silence the minority in their ranks who have the courage to challenge these absurd claims and the policies they make possible?

Need examples?

Each of the Emergency Use Authorizations for three Covid injections currently being distributed in the US said quite clearly that there was no evidence that the treatments could or would curb transmission, something that has been eloquently borne out in a boatload of studies on so-called breakthrough cases in the last 2-3 months.

Yours truly, that faithful peasant trafficker in "trivia," read these EUAs immediately when they were issued in December of 2020 and January of 2021 and wondered how this salient fact was compatible with a vaccine rollout clearly anchored in the idea that individual jab-taking was the best, indeed, the only way to "protect us all" through herd immunity.

Did any of the tens of thousands of doctors out there relentlessly pushing the injections in the name of collective responsibility ever read those summaries of clinical efficacy on transmission?

If they did not, they are professionally negligent and thus undeserving of any further deference or respect.

If they did and continued to state or imply that the injections would halt infection and transmission, then they should be held responsible for the deaths and injuries caused in those taking the injections under this misleading premise.

And if and when the apartheid vaccine passport system ever comes, as it should, under prosecutorial scrutiny, these same doctors should be right there in the dock with the politicians as accessories to the crime for providing a completely bogus intellectual underpinning for the freedom-killing project.

Where were all these brilliant minds as the wholly captured CDC and FDA, throwing one of the most elemental premises of immunology casually out the window, repeatedly cast doubt upon the reality and potency of natural immunity, and serially suggested that a not fully-tested vaccine that only produces antibodies for a part of the virus provides better protection than the body's own millenary defenses?

Did they protest it? Or at least have the temerity to mock the outright idiocy of such statements and suggestions? Did they stop and ask whether that made any sense? Outside of a brave minority, very few did, or indeed, do so now.

Most of them acted like a physician I know who, after receiving a stack of studies from a patient regarding the potency and durability of natural immunity (none of which he had read or even heard of) along with a request for a statement attesting to the patient's recovery from Covid, literally ran out of the room for 15 minutes, only to return with a mealy-mouthed and gaslighting statement that in no way confirmed his patient's recovery, nor the now scientifically undeniable fact of his ample protection from the worst effects of the virus.

Where are the protests from these people who until a few years ago could be heard pontificating about the "sacred nature" of the doctor-patient relationship and the "doctrine of medical necessity" now that those seminal concepts of medical ethics are being torn to shreds by vaccine mandates that make no distinctions between individual patient susceptibilities to the disease?

Have these bathetic citers of Hippocrates begun to think about what this could mean down the road for the practice of medicine? After having cheered government efforts to foist experimental injections on tens, and more probably, hundreds of millions of people for whom these injections can do no statistically significant good, and thus only harm, they are in no position to stop further pharmaceutical demands from the combined forces of big business and government.

On what basis, for example, could a doctor now object on behalf of his patient to an employer who, waving a statistical model produced at some Pharma-financed institute, has decided to mandate the universal prescription of, say, statins, or more ominously, antidepressants among the workforce in the name of reducing mortality, absenteeism or simply bringing down insurance costs?

In such a case, a large percentage of that workforce would be taking drugs they do not need. But after having folded in the face of efforts to do the same with medications of much less proven efficacy and completely unknown side effects, why would corporate backers even consult the doctors in the future?

The sad truth is that they won't.

Finally, we must reassert what is arguably one of the greatest—if most assiduously ignored—responsibilities of a healer: the obligation to calm and reassure the patient.

Where were the doctors when it came to telling their patients that statistically proven chances of dying from Covid were minimal, about the same as dying from the flu? Where were those who repeatedly pointed out the steep age and comorbidity gradient among the disease's mortal victims?

Again, with honorable exceptions, these mostly very well-paid practitioners have been completely AWOL; that is, when they have not been eagerly using their state medical boards to harass and sanction those of their colleagues with the temerity to point out these inconvenient truths.

Worse yet, many of them chose to further lie and insult us with blatantly false bromides about how Covid is a "threat to all" that "doesn't discriminate among its victims."

Certain Jesuits of my acquaintance often used to say, "To whom much is given, much is expected." During the middle years of the 20th century, the social privilege, deference and power previously granted to clerics, and then to writers, was bequeathed to the science-based healers.

While they have done much to improve our lives with the money and authority we have given them, they have—even though they seem largely unaware of it—now fallen into a grave state of moral decadence.

If more had, like their early 20th century predecessors, been forced to study and acknowledge the always present threat of hubris in human affairs, they might have been able to head off this historical denouement.

Sadly, however, most today are unreflective technocrats unable to recognize, never mind critique and distance themselves from, the ever more limiting epistemologies within which they carry out their daily tasks. And because of this Oedipal blindness, they will soon, much sooner than most of them think, lose much of the social capital they had assumed was theirs to wield in perpetuity.

26 October 2021

ELITE CONTROL THROUGH THE
ADMINISTRATION OF "SOCIAL DEATH"

ecember 3rd, 2010 may very well go down as an important turning
point in the history of human governance.

On that day, PayPal decided to permanently block Wikileaks'
ability to receive donations for its investigative journalism project, rooted
in the judicious sourcing and publication of leaked government and
industry documents.

With this decision, the globe-spanning cash management service
abandoned any pretense that it did, could, or would operate free of the
dictates of the US-led international security consensus.

Rather, it allowed all the world to see what a very small minority
of analysts had been saying quite regularly since the 1990s: that the
explosive upward trajectory of Silicon Valley technologies—with their
unprecedented ability to surveil private citizens and to control the flow
of money and information into their lives—can only be understood in
terms of its initial and ongoing relationship to the US Deep State and
its NATO and Five Eyes servants.

Unfortunately, very few people took note of the December 2010
announcement and its future implications for our lives.

The practice of ostracism—we get the term from Ancient Greece—is
as old as the history of organized human societies. Powerful political
actors and their courtiers have always despised the minority within the
society who raise questions about their competence or legitimacy, and
thus generally have had few compunctions about visiting exile, or if
needed, physical death upon them.

It was not until the late Middle Ages that this elite impunity began to
be substantially challenged. In 1027, for example, at a gathering known
as the Peace and Truce of God, a group of Catalan priests, commoners

and small landowners came together to challenge the feudal nobility's right to use coercive violence against them. More well known today is the English *Magna Carta* of 1215 which established *habeas corpus*; that is, the sovereign's obligation to explain in writing why and where he was imprisoning each one of his subjects.

It was from these humble challenges to sovereign power that modern democracy—understood as a system where those few wielding political power derive their prerogatives from the many, and thus must respond to their desires—was developed.

Among those who grew up during and just after the antiwar movement's *de facto* defeat of the military-industrial complex's war on Vietnam, this inherently tension-laden relationship between elite power and popular consent was widely understood.

Conversely, this celebration of "people power," as it was sometimes called back then, was viewed with deep fear and suspicion by the agents of the US national security elite which, under the cunning leadership of Allen Dulles and others, had insinuated itself into the inner reaches of the US presidency during the Truman and Eisenhower administrations.

These unelected elites viewed the United States as an empire, and understood that no empire could ever grow and prosper as such if it were to in any way grant the common people a check on their "right" to intimidate and inflict violence upon other countries.

So while many citizens of the country basked in the apparent reaffirmation of their fundamental rights and liberties during the late 1970s and 1980s, the recently chastened agents of the Deep State got back to work.

The first move in this claw-back effort was Ronald Reagan's decision to name William Casey, one of the last remaining links to the foundational Dulles years at the CIA, to head that same organization. More fundamental still was the national security establishment's decision to promote and execute "demonstration wars," which is to say conflicts of limited geopolitical importance, but of potentially large psychological value, in Grenada, Panama and the Persian Gulf over the next decade.

The first and most obvious of these psychological goals was to remind the world of the US desire and ability to project power wherever and whenever it deemed it necessary to do so. The second, especially important after both the external and internal defeats handed to the war-making elites over Vietnam, was to re-habituate the US public to the necessity and the supposed nobility of making war.

The third and arguably most important goal, which is deeply inter-twined with the last objective mentioned, was to experiment with new methods of putting the media back into the government-controlled pocket it had managed to crawl out of in the late 1960s and much of the 1970s. Indeed, as Barbara Trent's superb *Panama Deception* suggests, this was arguably the prime goal of the attack on that Central American country.

As George Bush Sr. (engaging in the erstwhile elite practice of giving away to those listening carefully the real nature of their aims) exultantly declared in the wake of the premeditated destruction of Iraq and the fiery death of several hundred thousands of its inhabitants: "By God, we've kicked the Vietnam Syndrome once and for all."

The government's reaction to the attacks of September 11th, centering on the promulgation of what appears to have been a largely pre-prepared Patriot Act, ushered in the next act of the great Deep State revenge tour: the near wholesale inversion of the citizen's relationship to the state.

In the name of "fighting terrorism," we were all reclassified, in effect, as "guilty until proven innocent," with the government now arrogating to itself in the generalized absence of probable cause, the right to snoop on all our private communications, to create elaborate profiles of our daily comportments and to search our cars without warrant at airports and at an ever-growing list of other so-called sensitive areas. And they did so without widespread citizen resistance.

In the first decade of this century, the same US Deep State took advantage of the implosion of mainstream journalism's business model to greatly extend its ability to direct and control public opinion in the US and Europe.

Emblematic of this transformation was the sweeping Americaniza-tion in the geopolitical and cultural focus of Europe's so-called "quality dailies" during this period, something which in turn greatly enhanced the Atlanticists' ability to publicly and concertedly disparage any political actor who raised the slightest objections to NATO's strategic goals, or the EU's financial and culture-planning aims.

All of which brings us back to Julian Assange. When he revealed the grotesque and heartless nature of US war crimes in Iraq in graphic detail, the Deep State decided that a mere campaign of character assassination of the type used with those foreign leaders who question the core goodness of the US or its policies would not do. Rather, it needed to visit complete social death upon him. And thanks to PayPal and all of the other high-tech platforms that followed its lead, it has been able to do so quite successfully.

A decade later the techniques of public-private thuggery employed to socially assassinate Assange and end his program of independent journalism are being broadly used against large swathes of the US population.

With Covid, the US government, working in concert with the almost wholly co-opted corporate press now vigorously pursues anyone questioning the logical coherence of the Covid narrative with well-orchestrated campaigns of defamation. (Remember the fate of those two emergency room doctors from California who questioned the severity of the disease in the Spring of 2020?).

And when numerous medical figures of much greater scientific renown, such as John Ioannidis and the Nobel Prize winner Michael Levitt to name just two examples, similarly questioned the core suppositions of the Covid narrative, the now rock solid government-media-high-tech alliance summarily banished them from most platforms.

It appears that the Biden Administration—or perhaps more accurately, the combination of Deep State, Big Pharma and international finance potentates currently designing its policies—might have actually believed these tools of coercion would be sufficient to achieve their goal of turning every man, woman and child in the country into a perpetual vaccine patient, and blissful donor of ever greater amounts of their personal information for commercial exploitation and enhanced state and corporate control over their lives.

But as it became increasingly clear in the late spring and summer of 2021 that the campaign of informational terror was no longer effectively delivering the desired results on the vaccine front, the US government turned, as they had in the case of Assange, to their corporate allies and the option of inflicting social death on those who continued to believe that their bodies and their lives belonged to themselves and not the government and its Big Pharma backers.

And let's be honest and not shy away from the truth. This is exactly what is going on.

After quite consciously using the enormous moral and rhetorical force of the government and media to label a third to a half of its own citizens as social pariahs, the Biden Administration is now working hand-in-glove with the country's large corporations to destroy these same people's standing as fully empowered citizens through the destruction of their livelihoods.

And this, to impel people to take a vaccine that clearly does not do the first thing a vaccine must always do: prevent transmission of disease.

And don't be fooled by the fact that the orders to socially assassinate millions of our fellow citizens are delivered in seemingly rational tones, and presented as a wholly logical and unremarkable approach to controlling Covid by the media.

Like all flailing empires before it, ours has come home and loosed its ever-ghoulish and ever-paranoid furies upon its own people.

It is a truly frightening spectacle.

But as students of history we can take heart in the fact that even as campaigns like the one now being waged against at least one-third of the US population in the name of safety cause untold amounts of heartache and destruction, they are seldom successful in the long run.

People eventually decide that living life in constant fear is to not live at all, and find their way back to the sacred practice of affirming life, with all its risks and disappointments, at every turn.

10 November 2021

VACLAV HAVEL AND THE SEMIOTICS
OF PUBLIC MASKING

For me, one of the worst inventions of the contemporary university is political science, a discipline that, with its mainly presentist and transactionalist orientation, tends to dramatically minimize the always very intimate relationship between politics and culture, especially the cardinal importance that public rituals have in every effort to radically reorient the operational concepts of reality among the citizenry

When, in his speech to the US Congress 31 years ago, Vaclav Havel said that "consciousness precedes being, and not the other way around," he spoke not only as a politician, but as a man of culture, and more specifically, a man of the theater, a place where the semiology of the stage is often as important as the words that come out of actors' mouths.

Thirteen years earlier, in the most decadent years of the Soviet period in Czechoslovakia, Havel wrote "The Power of the Powerless," an essay in which he uses his very detailed understanding of the symbolic codes of the stage to explain certain mechanisms of the system of oppression then in force in his country.

He focuses his exposition on a fictional manager of a fruit and vegetable store who every morning puts a sign in the window of his shop that says "Workers of the world, unite!" The playwright then wonders to what extent this gentleman and people passing by the sign believe in the words found on it. He concludes that the vast majority of them probably don't think much, if at all, about its content. Then, referring to the greengrocer, he goes on to say:

"This does not mean that his action had no motive or significance at all, or that the slogan communicates nothing to anyone. The slogan is really a sign, and as such contains a subliminal but very definite message. Verbally, it might be expressed this way: 'I, the greengrocer XY, live here and know what I must do. I behave in the manner expected of me. I can be depended upon and am beyond reproach. I am obedient and therefore have the right to be left in peace.' This message, of course, has an addressee: it is directed above, to the greengrocer's superiors, and at the same time it is a shield that protects the greengrocer from potential informers."

In this way, according to Havel, the greengrocer is saved from a confrontation with himself, and the feelings of humiliation that this inner encounter would bring on:

"If the greengrocer had been instructed to display the slogan 'I'm scared and therefore I'm unquestionably obedient' he would not be nearly so indifferent to its semantics even though the statement would reflect the truth. The greengrocer would be embarrassed and ashamed to put such an unequivocal statement of his own degradation on display in the shop window, and quite naturally so, as he is a human being, and therefore has a sense of his own dignity. To overcome his complication, his expression of loyalty must take the form of a sign which, at least on its textual surface, indicates a level of disinterested conviction. It must allow the greengrocer to say: 'What's wrong with the workers of the world uniting?' Thus the sign helps the greengrocer conceal from himself the base foundations of his obedience, while at the same time concealing the base foundations of power. It hides them behind the façade of something high. And that thing is ideology."

That Covid exists and has contributed to the deaths of many people is a fact. But the notion that it constitutes an unprecedented threat that requires the destruction of basic rights that have been hard-won over the centuries is an ideological presumption, one, moreover, that has been heartily disproven by reality in places like Sweden, Belarus and huge expanses of the so-called developing world.

Here are the age-stratified statistics of the Infection Fatality Rate (IFR) for the disease, recently compiled by John I. A. Ioannidis, one of the most prestigious bio-statisticians in the world.

30-39 0.031 percent (or a survival rate of 99,969 percent)
40-49 0.082 percent (or a survival rate of 99,918 percent)

50-59 0.27 percent (or a survival rate of 99.73 percent)
60-69 0.59 percent (or a survival rate of 99.31 percent)
More than 70, between 2.4 and 5.5 percent (or a survival rate
of 97.6 and 94.5 percent depending on residential situation)

Since the summer of 2020, masks have been held up by authorities all over the world as an essential element in fighting the spread of this supposedly unprecedented viral scourge. This, despite the fact that there is not much solid scientific evidence to prove that this is the case.

But as Havel reminds us, the masks' apparent lack of usefulness does not mean that they have "no motive or meaning."

No. Wearing the mask during Covid, like the apparently innocuous greengrocer's sign, sends very important messages. They might be summed up in the following way:

"I accept that we are living in very special times that require that the authorities, who always know more than me, must have a free hand to destroy the normal rhythms of life and of participatory democracy and that I, as a citizen, really have no right to disagree with their view of reality; that is, that I understand that I am no longer a citizen, but a subject. And I understand further that my mask serves as a shield against the attacks of the growing army of people in my neighborhood and on social media ready to accuse me of being less than interested in the feelings of others."

For Havel, the only solution for those in such an environment who really want to live in freedom and dignity is to stop giving passive or active consent to all the ideological lies in the social theater around them, and to instead embrace life. He writes:

"Between the aims of the post-totalitarian system and the aims of life there is a yawning abyss: while life, in its essence, moves towards plurality, diversity, independent self-constitution, and self-organization, in short, towards the fulfillment of its own freedom, the post-totalitarian system demands conformity, uniformity, and discipline. While life strives to create new and unlikely structures, the post-totalitarian system contrives to force life into its most probable states ..... Ideology, in creating a bridge of excuses between the system and the individual, spans the abyss between the goals of the system and the goals of life. It pretends that the requirements of the system derive from the requirements of life. It's a world of appearances trying to pass for reality."

To reject the ideological schemes of "reality" imposed from above and to instead embrace the most true and fundamental impulses of life is precisely what conviction-driven pilots, nurses, teachers, policemen, lawyers, parents, and many others are doing right now before the tyranny of mask and vaccine mandates.

They understand much better than those noisy and nosy elites—who before February 2020 loved to quote Foucault on biopolitics and rail against the often voluntary use of veils in the Islamic world, but who now only care now about imposing semiotic and physical obedience on everyone—that what Bergson called *élan vital* at the beginning of the 20th century is the root of all healthy human fulfillment.

And were he were still with us, I'd like to believe Havel, the great scholar of theater and social semiotics, would have no problem correctly identifying our current mask theater as the destructive and repressive farce that it is, and those that refuse to play along as the bearers of light, and the custodians of the creative energies we will need to reconstruct and sustain freedom in the world.

16 November 2021

A NOTE TO MY WELL-CREDENTIALED FRIENDS

I t really isn't that complex.

The injections you and many others were dragooned into taking under the threat of losing your job and your basic civil liberties do not protect you from getting Covid or passing it on.

Nor have they liberated you from mask-wearing, social distancing, the ongoing threat of lockdowns, and helpful advice from the government on how, and with whom, you can socialize at Christmas.

Among some age cohorts, the risks of serious adverse effects from the injections are higher than from those from Covid.

Meanwhile, the mandates, track-and-trace rituals, and now bio-passports, continue to crush small enterprises and exclude huge swaths of minority populations from participation in public life.

The segregation in our major cities is palpable and becoming more entrenched. Classes and events in large Northeastern universities are being canceled due to rising cases, and this is despite high vaccination rates, quarantines and masking.

These draconian impositions have not given us our lives and freedoms back. They continue to grind down marginalized peoples not only in the US but all over the world.

It's all there to see for anyone disposed to going beyond the mental parameters established and enforced by legacy media.

So, the real questions at play here are psychological and spiritual ones.

And it can be summarized more or less in the following fashion.

Are you as a member of the well-educated Western elite class prepared to explore the possibility that members of the sociological cohort to which you belong are capable of highly organized evil and deception rooted in a deep disdain for the core humanity and inherent dignity of all people?

Are you open to imagining that people—to borrow a phrase much-loved in certain circles—"who look like you," live in "nice" neighborhoods like yours, and want all the markings of the good life for their children as you do, are also capable of monstrous deeds and the propagation of extremely damaging herd-induced stupidities?

Do you ever think of using the knowledge of history your prestigious education might have afforded you for something other than establishing favorable comparisons with the past that prop up the idea of Western man's triumphant march of progress and, of course, your sociological cohort's starring role within it?

For example, do you ever think about how Europe's best and brightest sent millions of people to senseless deaths between 1914 and 1918, well after it was clear that doing so would do nothing to achieve the announced objectives of the conflict, objectives which were themselves based on deeply flawed logic and analytical assumptions?

Or will you avoid all that by mentally invoking a key, if largely unstated, conceit of late modernity's meritocratic mind: that success within the games established to distribute elite power (such as entry into Ivied schools with big endowments and plum jobs in finance) confer upon the winners of these games a moral weight that effectively exonerates them from the type of scrutiny that they compulsively apply to other, "less accomplished" human beings?

This is a question that those of us fortunate to be reasonably well-educated, reasonably well-fed and reasonably well-sheltered must now urgently confront.

And the manner in which the majority of us choose to respond to it will go a long way toward determining the shape of the world our children and grandchildren will inherit from us.

17 December 2021

WE'VE LET THEM GET DEEP INSIDE OUR
HEADS AND OUR COMMUNAL LIVES

I don't know about you, but I long ago learned how to recognize when I was suffering from a cold or flu, and how best to prevent myself and others from suffering from its most deleterious effects.

I developed knowledge in this area by simply watching and listening to others, and then verifying these theoretical inputs against the observable reactions and comportments of my own body.

I do not think I am unique in this. I think that, if left to their own devices, most people can determine the difference between a sore throat with a runny nose and a malady that may be attacking their body in a more serious and systematic way.

Perhaps, I should correct myself. I believe that *until 22 months ago* most people could confidently engage in this time-honed process of discernment. Now I am not sure that is the case.

What has changed?

What has changed is that there has been a concerted psychological campaign to effectively insert abstract and often empirically ques-tionable paradigms of sickness *between* individual citizens and their understanding of their own bodies, paradigms expressly designed to remove the locus of control from that citizen and his or her instincts and deposit it in the hands of some combination of medical and governmental authority.

Viewed in terms of metaphors of sight, we could say that a distorting lens provided by outside forces that places a great emphasis on vulnera-bility and dependence rather than resilience is now mediating, and thus reconfiguring, the relationship that millions of people have with their own sense of health, as well as with their fellow citizens.

The mechanism used to effect for this massive usurpation of individual confidence and instinct was, of course, mass testing which conferred on the government and their chosen health officials what Gabriel García Marquez suggests in *One Hundred Years of Solitude* is one of the greatest cultural powers of all: the power to name.

What up until early 2020 was a set of symptoms referenced loosely and imprecisely under the rubric of "seasonal colds and flus" and expected to be lived as a perennial and unremarkable personal matter, has with the onset mass testing been given a specific name and imbued with an all-encompassing spectral presence.

Once again, the template used to create and justify the War on Terror is instructive here. Before the inception of that never-ending pretext for projecting US power, war largely concerned soldiers who were defined in terms of their oppositional relationship to civilians. The first were fair game as objects of attack, but the second, at least in theory, were not.

What the war on terror did was to basically redefine everyone in the world, including US citizens, as *potential soldiers* against all that was considered good and right by the US government. How was this done? By amassing intelligence on everyone—intelligence, of course, that only government officials had the ability to see and manipulate—we were all turned into suspects, or if you prefer, pre-criminals.

After all, is there any one of us whose being could not be made to appear suspicious and thus worthy of attack (be it in the form of character assassination, strategic maiming or outright legal entrapment) by a group of people with full editorial control of the most minute details of our personal lives?

Before the Spring of 2020, one was either sick or well according to long-understood empirical measures.

But with the advent of mass testing for asymptomatic people (with a test designed to generate copious false positives), and with it, the invention of the mythology of rampant asymptomatic transmission, the elites gained the instant ability to portray millions of us as "pre-sick," and thus as potentially grave threats to the general welfare.

And now the generalized suspicion and fear they hoped to develop in us is lodged deep inside most people's brains and is affecting family and community relations in very granular ways.

The results are all around us to see. A week ago, at Christmas I had a runny nose and sore throat. In past years, before such banal things had been given a name and imbued—in complete contradiction to all empirical evidence—with legendary powers of destruction, I would have made a personal decision, rooted in my knowledge of my body, and a common-sense understanding of the danger I might or might not pose to others, to go, or not to go, to the family gathering. And the family member hosting the party would have respected whatever I decided to do. Indeed, in all likelihood, he or she would never have been party to my internal deliberations.

But now, thanks to the web of pre-sickness detection supposedly enabled by a wildly inaccurate test, my sniffles were now a grave public matter. What if I was "positive" and passed it on to someone in their house? Then those people, who are constantly being "tried" for pre-sickness at their schools or places of work, would have to stay home for several days.

Totally obviated from the calculus in this scenario was the fact that these "positive" people might not even be at all sick as judged by empirical means, or whether—in the case my sniffles were somehow related to the now mythologized virus—his or her "catching it" could or would have any serious long-term effects on them, or their classmates or their fellow workers.

But now the only thing considered important is the school or workplace's "duty" to exercise segregation in the name of a vague and empirically unprovable notion of safety.

Another young adult family member tested positive near Christmas and was told by his employer to stay home.

He has been completely symptom-free now for at least a week. But he has still not been able to return to work. Why? Because the employer, deeply enmeshed in test-think and thus now completely unable to trust either my youthful relative's word or their own powers of observation, insists he must be able to first produce a negative test. Well, guess what? There are now virtually no such tests available in the whole metropolitan area where we live. And so he sits, fully healthy and unpaid in his apartment.

This is madness.

We are, under the pressure of what is arguably the most ambitious and well-coordinated perception management campaign in history, having some of our more basic perceptual and behavioral instincts rapidly bred out of our lives.

And worse yet, most people have yet to fathom or even contemplate the actual reasons why this is being done and, what it all portends for the future of human dignity and freedom.

The prime goal of all social elites is to gain and maintain their power. And for the most part, they are deeply aware of the expense and inefficiency of doing so through the constant application of physical force.

This is why they have, since the time of the Sumerians, spent enormous amounts of energy and money on culture-planning campaigns designed to achieve widespread docility among the general populace.

In short, the powerful know that creating cultural realities that allow them to "get inside the heads" of ordinary individuals and their families is the gold standard of power maintenance and extension.

Sadly, during the last 22 months millions of people around the world have not only not resisted these attempts to intrude on our individual and communal dignity, but have, in their weakened psychic state, effectively welcomed them into their lives with open arms.

And there they will stay, until more of us decide to reassume the basic responsibilities of adult sovereignty and vigorously cast them back into the dark warehouse of classic authoritarian techniques from whence they were pulled by politicians working at the behest of the Deep State, Big Capital, Big Pharma and Big Tech.

5 January 2022

IT WAS ALL THERE IN THE EUA.
WHY COULDN'T THEY SEE IT?

T he first thing I did when the three Covid vaccines were given their Emergency Use Authorizations between mid-December 2020 and late February of 2021 was to seek out the summaries of the clinical findings that had led to these regulatory actions. I quickly found them and delved into what they had to say on protection against infection and transmission.

I did so because my intuitions, backed by my reading of esteemed scientists blocked from appearing in the mainstream media, had long suggested to me that the endgame envisioned by those managing the pandemic was to impose vaccine mandates on as many people and as many populations as they could.

And I knew that the ability to successfully implement this plan of widespread vaccination would hinge, or at least should hinge, on the ability to substantiate the injections' effectiveness in the key realms mentioned above: preventing infection and transmission.

The first company to receive approval, and hence to have a briefing document issued about its product by the FDA, was Pfizer. Shortly after the document was published on December 10th 2020 I read it and zeroed in on the section titled **"Known Benefits"** (p.46) where I found the following three-line summary:

- Reduction in the risk of confirmed Covid-19 occurring at least 7 days after Dose 2
- Reduction in the risk of confirmed Covid-19 after Dose 1 and before Dose 2
- Reduction in the risk of confirmed severe Covid-19 any time after Dose 1

Hmm, that's funny I thought, there was nothing about the ability to do what government officials and media talking heads were clearly suggesting they would do: stop people from passing on the virus.

I kept on reading and came to another much longer section on **"Unknown Benefits/Data Gaps."** There I learned that there was not enough information from the limited trials to make any solid affirmative claims about:

- Vaccine Duration of protection
- Vaccine Efficacy with immunosuppressed populations
- Vaccine Effectiveness in individuals previously infected with SARS-CoV-2
- Vaccine Effectiveness in pediatric populations
- Vaccine effectiveness against asymptomatic infection
- Vaccine effectiveness against long-term effects of Covid-19 disease
- Vaccine effectiveness against mortality
- Vaccine effectiveness against transmission of SARS-CoV-2

And in the midst of all of these *de facto* admissions of their limits, I found the paragraph below—listed under the heading of **"Future vaccine effectiveness as influenced by characteristics of the pandemic, changes in the virus, and/or potential effects of co-infections"**—which seems to indicate that the makers of the vaccines and the regulators overseeing their efforts were well aware that any initial efficacy could quickly be rendered nil by the fast-mutating nature of the virus:

"The study enrollment and follow-up occurred during the period of July 27 to November 14, 2020, in various geographical locations. The evolution of the pandemic characteristics, such as increased attack rates, increased exposure of subpopulations, as well as potential changes in the virus infectivity, antigenically significant mutations to the S protein, and/or the effect of co-infections may potentially limit the generalizability of the efficacy conclusions over time. Continued evaluation of vaccine effectiveness following issuance of an EUA and/or licensure will be critical to address these uncertainties."

When I checked on the Moderna briefing document issued a week later, I found virtually the same set of disclaimers (starting on page 48) issued in virtually the same language. And when the FDA released the Janssen briefing document on February 26th 2021, there was yet another rehash (starting on page 55) of the same disclaimers in essentially the same idiom.

I was stunned. The issuance of these documents coincided with the kick-off of the vaccination campaign in which they were clearly being sold to the public on the basis of their ability to stop infection and transmission. To say the least, they were oversold by most of the top public-health officials and TV pundits, including most of the people relied upon as experts.

Is it, and was it, really plausible to believe that the officials who were leading the vaccine charge on this basis were unaware of what I found in an effortless internet search?

I would say no.

What thus disturbed me even more were the non-reactions I got from friends when I pointed them to the above-cited documents and asked them to observe the enormous gap between the known capabilities of the vaccines and what officialdom was saying they would do for us.

But even more surprising, if that is possible. is that not one reporter in the US that I know of ever confronted anyone in any of the government agencies with the contents of these easily retrievable and easily read documents.

What could explain this?

We know that the government and Big Tech have worked together to pressure reporters into not going where they don't want them to go. And this is certainly an important factor in ensuring a certain silence around these documents.

But I think there is a deeper dynamic driving this now persistent failure of so many people, especially the young, to confront authority with the documentary proof of easily-accessible facts. And it has a lot to do with an epochal change in the overall cognitive habits of our culture.

From Orality to Literacy...And Back Again

Thanks to scholars like Walter Ong and Neil Postman we have long been aware of how communicative technologies (e.g. printing presses, books, radio and television) can engender profound changes in our cognitive habits.

Ong explained in great detail what was lost and what was gained in the transition from a culture based primarily in orality to one primarily anchored in literacy, which is to say, the traffic of written texts. He notes, for example, that in the transition to widespread literacy we have lost much in the realm of appreciating the spoken word's embodied affective magic, and we have gained much in the realm of being able to translate experience into abstract concepts and ideas.

In his *Amusing Ourselves to Death* (1984) Postman argues that every communicative technology carries within it an epistemology, or worldview, that shapes and organizes our cognitive patterns, and from there, our operative concepts of reality. As he puts it, when trying to understand communication we must "start from the assumption that in every tool we create, an idea is embedded that goes beyond the function of the thing itself."

He goes on to suggest that the rise of a more or less stable representative democracy in the United States was inextricably linked to the fact that the country's late Colonial and early Republican periods were characterized, when compared to other previous societies, by an unusually wide and dense textual culture. Because we were a nation of obsessive readers, we were, he suggests, unusually well-equipped to visualize the many abstract ideas that one must assimilate to act responsibly and intelligently within a citizen-driven polity.

Postman believed, however, that electronic media, and especially television, were effectively supplanting this dense textual culture with an epistemology that, while not inherently better or worse, was fundamentally different in terms of its cultural emphases. Whereas reading encourages contemplation, linear thinking and as I have said, abstraction, television encourages entertainment, atemporality and the consumption of fleeting visual sensations.

He did not believe we could stop television's seductive appeal, nor should we try. He did, however, sustain that we can and should ask ourselves whether, and to what extent, the epistemological emphases of the medium are compatible with engendering the type of comportments we know to be essential for the creation of the civic good life in general, and functioning democratic politics in particular.

From what I can tell, we have not seriously taken him up on his suggestion which, if anything, appears to be even more urgent in the age of the internet, a technology that seems to only magnify and accelerate TV's epistemological emphases.

I have seen very concrete proof of this failure to address these important matters in my work as a professor.

About ten years ago, a completely new phenomenon entered my teaching life: students quoting words from my class lectures back to me in their written work. At first it was trickle that amused me. But with time, it morphed into a fairly standard practice.

Had I gotten that much more authoritative and captivating as a speaker? I very much doubted it. If anything, I had gone in the other direction, progressively replacing the classic "sage on the stage" method of exposition with an ever more Socratic approach to intellectual discovery.

Then it finally dawned upon me. The students I was now teaching were digital natives, people whose perceptions of the world had been shaped from the very start of their lives by the internet.

Whereas my first experiences of intellectual discovery, and those of most people coming of age during the half-millennium previous to my time on earth, had largely taken place in the solitary and contemplative encounter between reader and text, theirs had mostly taken place before a screen that tended to push often disparate and random sounds, images and short chains of text at them in quick succession.

As a result, reading, with its need for sustained attention and its requirement that one *actively imagine* for one's self what it is the writer is trying to say, was extremely challenging for them.

And because they cannot easily enter into dialogue with the written page, they had little understanding of the sense of power and self-pos-session that inevitably accrues to those that can and do.

Indeed, it seemed that many of them had already resigned themselves to the idea that the best a person could hope to do in this world of non-stop informational comets was to occasionally reach up to try and trap one long enough to give others the impression of being reasonably intelligent and in control of life. That education could be about something more than the game of serially defending the fragile self against a chaotic and vaguely threatening world—and instead be about something like actively building an affirmative and affirming personal philosophy— seemed, for many in this newer cohort, to be largely beyond their ken.

Hence, my newfound quotability.

In a world where all is fluid and most are driven by the search for fleeting sensations, and where establishing a personal hermeneutic through reading and contemplation is considered quaintly quixotic when not impossible, the mutterings of the authority figure nearby take on an enhanced attraction.

This is especially the case for the many young people who, through no fault of their own, have been raised to see almost all human relations as essentially transactional in nature. Since I "need" a good grade and the prof is the person who will ultimately be giving it to me, it certainly can't hurt to flatter the old goat. You know, give a little bit to get a little bit back.

What's all this have to do with the news coverage of the EUA reports mentioned above and so much more in the journalistic treatment of the Covid phenomenon?

I would suggest, though I obviously cannot be sure, that this outlook on information management is now predominant among many of the young and not so young people working in journalism today. Unfamiliar with the slow and deliberate processes of deep analytical reading and the importance of seeking information that lies beyond the frenetic and ever more highly managed jungle of delivered feeds, they find it very difficult to forge a durable, unique and cohesive critical praxis.

And lacking this, they, like many of my students, latch on to the oral summaries of reality provided by those presented to them as being authoritative. That these authority figures might be directly contradicting what is found in the most weighty decision-making factor in a society of laws—its written archive—seems never to occur to them. Or if it does occur to them, the idea is quickly suppressed.

Who am I, they seem to say, with my inexperience in mindful reading and research and thus deep insecurities about my own critical acuity to raise discordant questions in relation to the great and powerful men and women before me?

The answer to this query, one apparently too few of us teachers and parents have given them, is that they are citizens of a republic whose founders sought to prevent them from ever having to face a return to governance by edict, and who knew that developing individual critical criteria through independent reading and research, and using the knowledge gained from these activities to openly challenge established authority, is the best way to insure this end.

29 January 2022

THE LIMITED HANGOUT OF
THE MANDATERS

Yesterday, a number of important Democratic governors lifted the mask mandates in their states. Almost to a one, they cited the changes wrought by the fast moving and relatively mild Omicron variant of the SARS-CoV-2 virus as the prime reason for the change.

What none of them did was admit what "the Science" has shown for at least two decades, and has been clear through the last two years to anyone doing a modicum of independent research on the subject: masks have never been shown to fundamentally alter the spread of respiratory viruses within the general population.

What they *did* say almost to a one, like their counterparts in Great Britain, Denmark and other countries now dismantling previous Covid restrictions, was that the return to normality was greatly facilitated by the uptake of vaccines in the populations they currently govern.

Nearly a half-century ago, a man named Ron Ziegler held the position now occupied by Jen Psaki. Like all presidential spokespeople before and since he was a serial dissembler.

But back then there were still a few journalists at the Presidential court and beyond willing to do their jobs. And when one day in the midst of the Watergate scandal he used the passive voice construction "Mistakes were made" in an attempt to explain away obvious breaches of honesty and ethics committed quite *actively* by the Nixon Administration, he was roundly mocked by the press corps.

Today this type of non-apology apology, which caused a scandal then, has, however, become ubiquitous across our social landscape. And that's a shame.

Why?

Because real apologies and expressions of accountability are important. Without them, neither the apologizer nor the aggrieved party ever experiences what the ancient Greeks considered a cardinal element in human development and human relations: catharsis.

This is especially so in the case of government entities. Without admissions of guilt, the assumptions and premises undergirding their failed policies remain intact, lying fallow until such time as the government entity in question feels it opportune to deploy them again in the service of another misguided crusade.

This is what is currently occurring with the Covid hawks who have violated our fundamental rights time and again over the last two years.

These enemies of human dignity and freedom now realize that many of their former supporters among the citizenry feel exhausted, and in many cases, flat-out deceived.

At the same time, however, they do not want to permanently relinquish the powerful repressive tools they have acquired during the two-year state of exception.

The answer?

One part of it, already mentioned, is the limited hangout operation now being conducted regarding the use of masks in public. By relaxing these strictures while in no way addressing the fundamental fallacies upon which the masking policies were based, they ensure that mask mandates can be brought back when and if they deem it necessary to do so.

The second part, which is far more pernicious and consequential, is the effort to push a proposition that is at best quite tenuous in light of what actual scientific studies are currently revealing about vaccine efficacy: that without widespread injection uptake the virus would have never receded, and we would have thus never have gotten into a position to recover our freedoms.

Note the underlying logic here. We are not getting our freedoms back because they intrinsically belong to us and were unjustly stolen. We are getting them back because an important plurality of us have done what the "experts" and the "authorities" coerced us into doing.

With this approach there is no catharsis or healing, and certainly no acquisition of new wisdom and knowledge. What there is, is a sly reification of the infantilizing and anti-democratic ways of thinking that have predominated in our policy-making class throughout the pandemic.

Though many people, laboring under the mortal fear of being branded with the weaponized term of "conspiracy theorist," are reluctant to admit it, the central concern of policy-makers throughout the pandemic has not been the health of our communities, but rather gaining enhanced control over where we go and what we put into our bodies.

There is nothing more central to the idea and practice of freedom than bodily autonomy. It is the basal freedom from which all others are derived. Without it—as the history of slavery starkly reminds us—all other liberties are comparatively ornamental.

For this reason, we must vigorously oppose this organized attempt to present the vaccines, which have been delivered to millions under severe coercion, as a great, if not the greatest, hero of the pandemic film.

8 February 2022

WHAT AN HONEST VACCINE ROLLOUT ANNOUNCEMENT MIGHT HAVE LOOKED LIKE

E stablishing counterfactual arguments can be a very valuable intellectual exercise. Doing so helps us remember something that our current oligarchic media system desperately wants us to forget: that there are always alternatives to what they sell to us as *The Only Realistic Way Forward*™.

Articulating what might have been helps us recover and stimulate the moral and intellectual imagination we must constantly cultivate if we are to resist the many incipient tyrannies in our midst. After all, if they kill our ability to envision more dignified and life-affirming approaches to our common problems—as they seem to have successfully done with so many of our well-credentialed countrymen—then it's game over. They win.

It is in that spirit—one that Josep Maria Esquirol describes as "Intimate Resistance"—that I submit the following version of what a Vaccine rollout document would look like if the agencies charged with protecting our health actually saw us as something more than cattle to be directed into behaviors amenable to the bottom lines of Big Pharma and the goals of a Deep State ever more interested in exercising control over the most intimate rhythms of our lives.

The Would-be Announcement

Over the last year, the SARS-CoV-2 virus has caused numerous hospitalizations and deaths in our nation. While the number of Covid hospitalizations and deaths reported in the press often appear quite large, no one is quite sure what they actually are owing to a) the proven inaccuracy of PCR tests b) the decision of the CDC not to distinguish clearly between those that were hospitalized or died primarily because of the virus and those for whom it was an ancillary factor in a much more grave and complex panel of ailments.

It is also important to bear in mind that for all the media comparisons to previous pandemics like the Spanish flu of 1918, which is estimated to have claimed as many as 50 million victims worldwide across a broad set of age cohorts, the SARS-CoV-2 virus has been relatively mild, with an Infection Fatality Rate (IFR) fairly close to that of the yearly flu, and an age gradient for severe illness and death that is overwhelmingly tilted toward the aged and/or those already battling multiple maladies.

But, of course, every severe illness or death is a tragedy for the family affected by them. This is why we are pleased to now offer the US public three new experimental vaccines, brought to market on an extremely accelerated schedule as part of the Operation Warp Speed effort initiated by President Trump in 2020.

Initial trial results suggest that these new medications *may* help curtail the rates of severe illness and death among those most prone to the most negative effects of the SARS-CoV-2 virus. However, we must underscore that since those trials were dramatically shorter than those normally required by federal rules, excluding animal trials which are often conducted to gauge both the effectiveness and possible side effects of new medicines, we cannot give any solid assurances that this will be the case.

Facts you need to know:

1. These vaccines are being made available to the public under Emergency Use Authorizations (EUAs), a categorization that falls considerably short of "Approval" owing to the drastic foreshortening of the trial process mentioned above. Therefore any claim that the vaccines are "safe and effective" must be seen not as factual, but rather aspirational. We will only be able to arrive at definitive conclusions about their effectiveness and safety in several years' time when the full cycle of trials is completed and/ or government agencies have rigorously collated and analyzed the results of their widespread experimental use among the public.
2. According to the federal rules governing the deployment of

EUA products citizens have "the option to accept or refuse administration of the product" and to know about "the alternatives to the product that are available and of their benefits and risks." Additionally, the EEOC has made clear that, under the ADA, the Rehabilitation Act, and Other EEO Laws, employers cannot offer incentives for vaccine uptake that are in any way coercive.

3. These US government rules are grounded in the broader structure of international law relating to medical experimentation that grew out of the Nuremberg Principles articulated in the wake of widespread medical experimentation by Nazi doctors on human subjects which state clearly that in matters of medical treatment the "voluntary consent of the human subject is absolutely essential." In short, no medication can be forced upon a human being without his or her consent. As a key promoter of, and signatory to, the Nuremberg Principles, the US government is legally bound by the directives contained therein.

4. The US government has granted the three large pharmaceutical companies that have produced such vaccines complete immunity from liability for any damages they might cause to those who take them. Therefore, if these experimental vaccines in any way damage your health, or the health of a member of your family, you will have little or no legal recourse for gaining compensation.

5. The traditional attraction of vaccines to those making public health policies lies in their ability to turn the vaccinated person into a "dead end" for the virus. Vaccines that have the capacity to stop the chain of infection and transmission in this way are said to offer "sterilizing immunity." While some scientists have expressed the hope that by lowering viral loads in the bodies of those injected with these three products (itself a largely unproven supposition) infection and transmission might be attenuated, there is nothing in the clinical data currently available to substantiate this claim. In fact, in the summaries of the clinical data gathered as part of the government's original EUA documentation (Pfizer p.53, Moderna p.48, and Janssen p.55) all state clearly there is not enough information to make any such

assertions.

6. Given that the vaccines have shown no documented ability to block infection and transmission, the argument that one should get vaccinated to further the public good has little or no validity. Rather, the decision to take one of them should be seen as a purely personal one.

7. As mentioned above, the one area where the experimental vaccines appear to have shown some effectiveness is in limiting severe illness and death among the relatively small number of the people in the volunteer cohort who became infected with the SARS-CoV-2 virus. However, this apparent success must be weighed against the fact that in at least one of the trials, overall mortality was greater in the vaccinated group than in the control group. Moreover, the EUA documents produced by the FDA on the basis of information provided to them by the pharmaceutical companies demonstrate that none of the companies were willing to even suggest that the ability of the vaccines to curtail severe illness and death might last beyond a period of two months.

8. The rates of vaccine effectiveness currently circulating in the media (e.g. the much repeated 95 percent efficacy attributed to the Pfizer vaccine) do not, as many people seem to assume, refer in any way to the level of overall protection a person receives against becoming infected or passing on the virus. As we have seen, the companies have admitted that there was not enough clinical information to make any claims in these areas of vital public concern. So what do they refer to? When speaking about vaccine effectiveness, we can express it in two principal ways. The first is in terms of Absolute Risk Reduction (ARR). For example, in the case of the Pfizer trials the number of people who developed Covid in the control (unvaccinated) group was an already incredibly low 0.88 percent (162 of a total of 18,325 people). In the vaccinated group, the number of those developing the disease was 0.04 percent (8 out of a total of 18,198). When we calculate the difference between the two outcomes as a percentage we get an ARR of 0.84 percent. That is, you are 0.84 percent less likely

to develop Covid if you get the injection. And that "benefit" only holds, according to the statistics provided by Pfizer, for the first seven days after injection. So where does the famous 95 percent effectiveness claim come from? That's the expression of vaccine effectiveness in terms of Relative Risk Reduction (RRR); that is, the difference between 0.84 percent and 0.04 percent expressed as a percentage. Again, this is not, we believe it is safe to say, what most people in the public understand when they hear the mantra that the current vaccines are 95 percent effective.

Summary: We are glad that these vaccines have been made available to the public, as they may prove to be beneficial for a number of people for whom health profiles make especially vulnerable to severe sickness and death as a result of exposure to the SARS-CoV-2 virus.

However, it is important to underscore that these vaccines are experimental and that no one actually understands their full effectiveness nor the set of side effects they might induce. And should severe side effects develop, the vaccinated person will find him or herself without legal relief before the vaccine manufacturers.

Moreover, as the abbreviated clinical trials have shown, these are not sterilizing vaccines and thus no one can or should be coerced to taking them in the name of the "public good." And even if they were shown to serve the public good by stopping infection and transmission, US government regulations and international law clearly prohibit coercing the individual citizen into taking them.

We wish you the best of luck in making your own decision about what medications you choose to take into your body at this troubling time in our nation's history.

9 February 2022

A PRIORI SCIENCE IN THE
SERVICE OF POWER

From 1564 to 1966 the Vatican regularly published and updated its famous *Index Librorum Prohibitorum*, a list of books that were deemed to be off-limits to any right-thinking Catholic. The church's reasoning on this was simple. And it went something like this.

Given the inherent fallibility of human beings, it was important that the clerisy guard its flock against contact with "misinformation" derived from "unreliable sources" that might divert their hearts and minds from what should always be their prime goal: gaining eternal salvation through the intercession of God's institutional representation here on earth: the Church of Rome.

The creation and maintenance of the censorious *Index* was animated by what philosophers call *a priori* thinking; that is, a process of intellectual inquiry characterized by reasoning absent evidence from first principles. It works for mathematics, geometry, and other disciplines rooted in logical deduction. Applied to natural sciences, humanities, anthropology, politics, and history, however, it speaks to a desperate desire to justify the status of previously determined "truths" that fortify a particular and often highly self-interested view of reality.

As is so often the case, the timing of the decision to create this official list of impure and dangerous readings was no accident.

For nearly a thousand years prior to the inception of the *Index*, the lettered functionaries of the papacy had exercised a near total monopoly over how its vast and largely illiterate flock could interpret and visualize the designs of the Almighty.

However, all that began to change when, in the middle of the 15th century, Johannes Gutenberg perfected the technology of movable type. From this moment onward books—and more specifically the Bible—which up until that time could only be reproduced by hand and was thus available to a very limited slice of the population, suddenly became a more or less widely available consumer item. Over the next half-century the numbers of those able to read, and to thus develop their own shadings of God's intentions, grew exponentially.

It was in the midst of this new "do-it-yourself" intellectual ferment that Martin Luther generated his *Ninety-Five Theses*, which would forever change the relationship between the commoner and state power in Western Europe.

To say that in issuing his critique Luther was taking on Rome would certainly be correct. But it would also be woefully incomplete, for Rome was in many fundamental ways a political appendage—and at the same time an essential symbolic guarantor—of the era's unquestioned political, social and economic superpower: a Spanish-led Habsburg Empire.

In other words, to question the power of Rome was not a mere theological gambit, but also a deeply political one that struck at the very roots of a vast network of interlocking interests stretching from South, Central and North America, on to Spain as well as much of today's Belgium, Holland, Italy, and Austria.

Aware that the uncontrolled spread of Luther's critique would seriously damage the cohesion of this enormous bundle of interests, the Church, working hand-in-glove with its Spanish Habsburg patrons, inaugurated the Council of Trent in 1545.

The goal of this 18-year long series of high-level meetings was quite clear: to coordinate a vast propaganda effort designed to centralize governance, codify and enforce liturgical rituals, restrict the circulation in Europe of the emergent intellectual currents of Protestant thought (with their relatively strong emphasis on individual conscience and textual reasoning), and to establish new, more sensually appealing iterations of what it meant to live in the grace of a Catholic god.

While it is always dangerous to make definitive judgments on the broad course of history, subsequent events would seem to suggest the Counter-Reformation launched in Trent, while fomenting the production of some of the most beautiful art the world has ever seen, ultimately fell short of its prime political goals.

During the succeeding centuries, the train of social and political progress in Europe, and the West more broadly, would for the most part be driven by those countries—as Weber famously suggested in the particular realm of economics—that had embraced the relatively more individualistic and rational-textual ethos of Protestantism.

In short, for all of the vigorous efforts of brainy proselytizers like the Jesuits, the pre-packaged truths of the Church could not compete with the thrill that many people were now deriving from reading and arriving at their own conclusions about the world and the workings of the heavens above.

For the last seven decades the US, like Habsburg Spain of the early 16th century, has lived a rather charmed existence, rooted in the fact that they were the only allied power to escape the ravages of war on their own soil.

And like the Spaniards who surged to global prominence on the basis of a largely accidental encounter with—at least to their eyes—a pillage-ready continent overflowing with natural resources, they convinced themselves that their good fortune was really the result of their unique moral virtues. And its leadership class worked assiduously, as the Jesuits would do after Trent, to create the sense among the homeborn population and the rest of the world that God truly did favor us more than any collective on the face of the earth.

Indeed, during the first four decades after WWII, it was easy for those living within the US cultural system to believe that this was, in fact, the case. In many ways, and I say this as someone who came of age in that sweet spot between the end of Vietnam and the inception of financialized capitalism, we truly *were* perhaps more free than any group of young people in the history of the world.

But while we saw that freedom as a perpetual right, the country's economic and social elites saw it as a conditional gift, one that could only be extended to us as long as their "right" to constantly increase their wealth and power remained undiminished.

By the mid 1990s, as the rest of the world finally began to catch up to the US in terms of economic productivity and living standards, it was clear that the elites' "rightful" returns on investment were shrinking and that something would have to give.

Playing with new financial instruments to spur wealth can only benefit so many for so long. And while the media did its best to convince Americans that all were, in fact, benefiting from the newly charged Wall Street casino, the realities of Main Street were telling people a very different story. That common citizens could, thanks to the Gutenberg-like effect of the early internet, begin to create ever more accurate narratives of what was being done to them, only heightened their sense of anger and betrayal.

Faced with the growing disenchantment of its citizens, the government and its allies in Big Finance began setting up the machinery they believed they would need to quell the inevitable rise of popular dissent down the road.

When we examine them closely, we can see that the invasions of Panama and Iraq in the early 1990s were, above all, experiments in domesticating the media. The crisis following September 11th was used to accustom people to heretofore unfathomable and flatly unconstitutional intrusions into the private realm of their lives, something I am reminded of each time I pass the huge sign saying "All Cars are Subject to Search" as I approach the departure drop-off point at Hartford's Bradley Airport.

With the Covid crisis, the Power Elites have gone in for the kill, seeking to deprive us all of the most basic of our freedoms, the one from which all others are derived: the right to decide what we will put into our bodies.

That so many people, especially on the left where the rhetoric of bodily sovereignty has long been used to defend a woman's right to an abortion, cannot see the fundamental nature of the struggle we are in is nothing short of astonishing... and is, sad to say, a tribute to the extremely well-executed nature of their propaganda drive to banalize and relativize the essential nature of the freedoms we once enjoyed.

But there is hope. And it comes from observing the incredible intellectual poverty of those now running the culture-planning machine at the highest levels of government and business and from seeing how reflexively they now recur to *a priori* reasoning when attempting to convince us to follow their lead.

The examples before us are far too many to count. This week, for example, we found out that the Centers for Disease Control and

Prevention has been hiding information about vaccine efficiency and safety out of a fear, according to that organization's spokesperson, that releasing it might allow some in the general public to misinterpret it as demonstrating that the vaccines—which by any standard clinical metric for such things are highly ineffective—are, you guessed it, highly ineffective.

There you have it in a nutshell.

Just like the Catholic hierarchy of the 16th century which decided that salvation could only be achieved through the intercession of the Church of Rome, and that therefore all intellectual activity must affirm this premise, the great mass of our politicians and public health authorities long ago decided that the only goal currently worth achieving is insuring the subjugation of as many bodies as possible to their dictates, and that all discussion around public health should thus militate toward that end.

This approach is, of course, massively dishonest and arrogant.

But most of all, it's pitiful, for it speaks to a leadership cadre that no longer believes in anything; that is, except a desperate desire to hold on to power.

It speaks to a leadership cadre, that in the classic pattern of leadership cadres presiding at times of epochal change, seeks refuge in the mythologies produced by, and circulated within, their own very narrow circle of similarly socialized adepts, a small circle they tend, sadly, to mistake as being truly representative of the population as a whole.

It speaks to a leadership cadre that, in its narcissistic madness, assumes everyone else, especially the less credentialed, is just as crazy and spiritually barren as they are and cannot perceive the vast gap between their *a priori* "truths" and observable reality.

It speaks, in the end, to a leadership cadre that knows in its heart of hearts that it has absolutely nothing to offer us, and strongly suspects, moreover, that its present prominence and power are the product of a long-running bluff and that, like all bluffs theirs will collapse as soon as enough people of conscience and empirical rigor stop running from their own shadows, turn around, and begin laughing derisively in their frightened and inauthentic faces.

24 February 2022

FOR DRS. WALENSKY AND
OFFIT: IT'S ALL IN GOOD FUN

Developing psychic detachment can be an important skill, one that is not always easy to attain. We are, in many ways, primitive creatures, driven by immediate concerns. Psychic detachment is the art of using both the will and the abstracting powers of the brain to put a brake on those often quite natural and pressing drives and concerns.

The advantages of doing so are widely recognized. We know, for example, that to stop and reflect in this way can save us from numerous destructive practices, from overeating and drinking to permanently alienating those we need or love.

We also know it is of great utility in what are sometimes referred to as the knowledge industries, a set of pursuits that, in one way or another, task us with generating essentializing representations of one aspect or another of the world's unfathomable complexity.

What we tend not to talk about and recognize as clearly are the sometimes deleterious effects of this same attribute. Among the numerous primary drives that the abstracting mind can blunt is the human tendency toward empathy. When we see and hear pain we generally react to it subrationally, moving, for example, on reflex to pick up the child who has fallen and is crying on the sidewalk before us. In other words, like so many other human properties, psychic detachment is a mixed bag.

And yet it is not always treated as such in the more credentialed sectors of our population. There, it often seems that the ability to think in highly abstract terms and to, in effect, banish the plight of individual human beings and their real life dramas from one's decision-making calculus is not only tolerated, but effectively lionized.

This trend has gone so far that we now see public figures speaking about policies that they have created and effectively imposed on other relatively powerless people acting, at times, as if they had nothing to do with creating them, and as if the human tragedies generated by them merit little or no concern.

I was recently reminded of this growing tendency toward moral flippancy in our elites as I watched interviews with two of the more influential architects of current US vaccine policy, Dr. Paul Offit and CDC chief Dr. Rochelle Walensky.

At one point in his extensive interview with a fellow physician named Zubin Damania, whose podcast handle is ZDoggMD, and with whom he appears to be quite chummy, Offit is asked about the important matter of natural immunity and its relation to the current Covid vaccinations.

To his credit, he goes against the shameful lies and obfuscations of the CDC and the FDA, and affirms natural immunity's long-established and uncontroversial standing in the field of immunology.

In response to Zdogg's assertion that data is showing that natural immunity is "pretty good" he says that this is:

"As you would expect. It's true for every other virus with the arguable exception of the flu. If you've gotten measles, there is no reason to get a measles vaccine, or mumps or rubella or chickenpox [vaccine]. I mean, you've been vaccinated essentially....It is not at all surprising that if you've been naturally infected that you will develop high frequencies of memory B and T cells which should protect you against serious illness. And I think that is what the CDC now has shown."

He then goes on to tell, between self-satisfied smiles of his own and giggles from Zdogg, how he was one of five people (the other four being Fauci, Vivek Murthy, Rochelle Walensky and Francis Collins) asked to advise the Biden administration on whether "natural infection should count in situations where the vaccine is mandated.." He says that he was one of two voices in the group that said it should, but that he lost.

But no sooner does he say this than, again amidst big smiles on both sides of the podcast, he tells how funny and silly it was that "sweet" Vivek Murthy—you know, the one who just asked Big Tech to collaborate in ratting on US citizens who dare to disagree with government vaccine policy—had asked everyone at this meeting of uber-important and publicly-known scientists to identify themselves by name before beginning the deliberations.

Ha-ha. Isn't that funny?

I guess it is when you are so pleased with yourself for being up there in the societal cockpit, and so well-practiced at psychic distancing that you can't even begin to think about the importance of your oh-so-jolly meeting of notables and its decisions on the lives of millions of people.

Hey Paul, did you ever think of taking a principled stance and going public with what you knew to be true about natural immunity? Did you ever think of challenging and exposing the blatant lies that both the CDC and FDA were then making up about it? Did you ever think of the millions of perfectly healthy people who, quite rationally, might object to taking an experimental medication that, according to your own words, they manifestly don't need?

Did you ever think of the cruelty bordering on sadism of forcing millions of people who, thanks to natural immunity posed no infectious threat to anyone, were having to choose between taking a medication that can do them little good and might do them considerable harm, and losing their livelihood?

No, for pleased-as-punch-with-himself Paul, it was nothing more and nothing less than a fun little chat between special folks like himself. And if Paul knows anything, it's that you don't get anywhere in life being principled and headstrong among the powerful. No, only "loser" hotheads, unable to see where power lies and laugh on cue at "sweet" Vivek's quirky brand of social etiquette do things like that.

A few days back Rochelle Walensky was invited to give an interview at her alma mater, Washington University in St. Louis. The first part of the discussion pivoted around softball questions which allowed her to pontificate on her decidedly woke and race-infused views of public health. It was more than halfway into the interview before her interlocutor finally got around to asking her about where she and the CDC might have gone wrong in their management of the Covid epidemic.

Here is what followed.

First, she told of how pleased she was when she heard (from a "CNN feed" no less) about the "95 percent effectiveness" of the vaccines because, like all of us, she just wanted to get the pandemic behind us.

And then she expresses, between chuckles, her shock upon learning that the vaccines might diminish in effectiveness over time "Nobody said waning...Nobody said what if the next variant...what if it's not as potent against the next variant?"

You see, even though a humanities professor like me with no scientific training knew —thanks to my readings of the Moderna, Pfizer and Janssen briefing documents, numerous scientific papers on vaccine effectiveness and safety, as well as from listening to people like Sucharit Bkahdi, Geert Vande Bossche and Michael Yeadon—by very early 2021 that the vaccines probably would not prevent transmission and might actually promote new resistant varieties of the virus, none of this was conceivable or knowable to the Director of the CDC.

Like the human hologram she apparently is, we are led to believe that she was there, but she was not really there. She was responsible, but really someone else was. "No one could have known," she exclaims, except, of course, the hundreds of thousands of us amateurs who did, in fact, know, and were censored and called science-hating anti-vaxxers for our troubles.

And of course, holograms don't do guilt or responsibility. Did she express any sympathy for the people that were forced out of jobs over their refusal to take what we now know, and she admits, were largely ineffective vaccines?

Nope, again even though she was in the chair, it was, of course, all beyond her control. And as a powerless spectator just like you and me, she was disappointed and surprised. Mistakes were made. She meant well. Her only real faults, as she said in the same talk, were the clearly well-intentioned ones of having "too little caution and too much optimism."

And while she was exonerating herself, she made time to give the masses a little bitty sermon on the nature of science itself.

Remember Science™?

That thing that was settled and brooked no dissent and was best represented by the guidelines published by the CDC, guidelines that the same organization encouraged employers and organizations of all types to use as a cudgel against those daring to think that bodily sovereignty was still fundamental freedom. That thing that "sweet" Vivek Murthy presently wants to conduct inquisitions about with the help of Big Tech.

Well here's what our hide and seek hologram said on that subject:

"And maybe the other thing I'll say is the gray area. I have frequently said, you know, that we're going to lead with the science. Science is going to be the foundation of everything we do. That is entirely true. I think the public heard that as science is foolproof, science is black and white. Science is immediate and we get the answers, and then we make the decision based on the answer. And the truth is science is gray, and science is not always immediate. Sometimes it takes months and years to actually find out the answer. But you have to make decisions in a pandemic before you have that answer."

Get it?

All those moves to censor and professionally destroy those who had opinions different from the CDC, actions rooted precisely in the presumption that science is, in fact, black and white, and that those who get it wrong need to be professionally punished, well, that's all a figment of your primitive imagination.

So yes, excessive psychic detachment that turns fellow human beings into self-referential objects of our own minds can be rather problematic. Indeed, I think, though I can't be sure, that psychologists even have a term to describe it: psychopathic.

10 March 2022

FACT-CHECKING AND THE
MAKING OF CULTURE

Social and political elites have long relied on euphemism to make their schemes of group control more palatable to those they see as their inferiors. Think here of "social distancing" or "mitigation measures" when they really mean forced separation and physical isolation.

Though such leaders pretend in certain moments to be comfortable with the use of brute force to achieve their desired domination of the masses, they are in reality quite frightened of going down that path, as they know that in an open conflict with the common people much can go wrong, and outcomes are anything but certain.

This is why they spend so much time and money on what Even-Zohar calls "culture-planning;" that is, arranging our semiotic environment in ways that naturalize schemas of social control that favor their interests, inducing in this way, what he calls "proneness" among considerable swathes of the population.

Why engage in conflict with the general population, with all that such conflicts portend in the way of unforeseen consequences, when you can teach people to welcome externally generated schemas of domination into their lives as gifts of benevolence and social improvement?

Though it is often forgotten, culture is derived from the very same Latin root, *colere,* that gave us the verb to cultivate. To cultivate is, of course, to engage in a conscious process of husbandry within nature, a process which, in turn, involves making repeated judgements about what one does and does not want growing, or even present, on a given patch of land.

Carrots and onions yes, weeds no.

Indeed, the very lack of specificity of the term weed tells us much about this process. Definitionally speaking, a weed has no inherent properties of its own. Rather, it is defined purely in terms of what it is not; that is, as something that the cultivator has deemed as having no positive use. In short, there is no such thing as a garden without value judgments regarding the relative utility of various species of plants.

The field of what we call culture (with a capital C) not surprisingly, obeys similar imperatives. Like species of plants, the stocks of information around us are nearly infinite. What turns them into culture is the imposition upon them of a man-made order that supposes the existence of coherent relations between and among them through structure-engendering devices like syntax, narrative and concepts of esthetic harmony.

And as in the case of our garden, human judgment and the power to enforce it—a mechanism sometimes referred to as canon-making—are fundamental to the process. Just as in farming, there is no such thing as culture without human discernment and the exercise of power.

So, if we seek to truly understand the cultural sea in which we swim and its effects on the way we view reality, we need to keep a close eye on the prime canon-making institutions in our cultural field (government, universities, Hollywood, Big Media, and Big Advertising) and constantly ask hard questions about how the vested interests of those that run them might affect the conformation of the cultural "realities" they place before us.

Conversely, those in power, and desirous of staying there, know that they must do everything in their control to present these cultural "realities" not as what they are—the result of quite conscious canon-making processes run by institutionally empowered elites—but as largely spontaneous derivations of the popular will, or even better, as mere "common sense."

New Technologies and Epochal Change

These efforts to convince the people that this is "just the way things are" can often be quite successful, and for surprisingly long stretches of time. Think, as we have seen, of how the Church of Rome used its stranglehold on the production of texts and large scale visual imagery to impose a largely uniform understanding of human teleology upon western European culture for the thousand years leading to the publication of Martin Luther's *Ninety-Five Theses* in 1517.

As I have suggested, the spread and subsequent consolidation of Luther's challenge to Rome would have been impossible without the invention of the technology of movable type by Gutenberg approximately a half-century earlier. Others before the monk of Wittenberg had sought to challenge Rome's monopoly on the truth. But their efforts foundered on an inability to spread their challenges to potential new adepts easily and quickly. The printing press changed all that.

Like Gutenberg's invention, the advent of the internet nearly three decades ago radically enhanced most common people's access to information, and from there, their comprehension of the important, and often nefarious role of canon-makers, or what we more commonly refer to as gatekeepers, in configuring operatives schemas of reality in their lives.

It is not clear whether those that decided to place this powerful tool at the disposal of the public in the mid-1990s anticipated the challenges it might pose to the ability to generate narratives amenable to the long-term interests of our entrenched centers of financial, military and social power. My guess is that they did, but that they assumed, perhaps correctly, that the ability to gather information about their own citizens through these same technologies would more than compensate for that potential danger.

And they had, I think, what they realized was one other very important card up their sleeve in their ongoing efforts to enhance their control of the public. It was their ability—as one participant in the Event 201 Covid simulation event from October of 2019 candidly put it—to "flood the zone" with information when they viewed it as necessary, generating in this way, an acute hunger in the population for top-down expert guidance.

Social Control Through Informational Scarcity….and also Informational Abundance

Up until the advent of the internet, elite-generated systems of narrative control pivoted, for the most part, on their ability to deprive citizens of information that might allow them to generate visions of reality that challenged "common sense" understandings of how the world "really works." And in the end, in fact, this remains their goal.

What is different today are the mechanisms they have developed to achieve this end.

No one, especially no one raised in a consumer culture where the individual's right to choose has been raised to a paramount social value, likes to be told that they cannot freely access this or that thing.

So how then can the elite culture-planner achieve the results of information control without setting off the alarms that frontal censorship would set off among the parishioners of the contemporary church of choice?

The answer—to go back to our metaphorical garden—is to seed the patch of land with weeds while its owner is away and return a short time later as a salesman bearing a new and completely effective cure against the plague that threatens his agricultural holdings.

Put another way, today's culture-planners are keenly aware of two things. One, that the initial liberatory jolt provided by the amount of information suddenly available through the internet has, for all but the most skilled and disciplined parsers of information, long since faded, and has been replaced by information overload, with the inchoate sense of confusion and dread that his condition carries with it. Two, that human beings are, as the history of agriculture and the multitude of other pursuits derived from its original organizational impulse demonstrate, order-craving creatures.

In this context, they know that if they want to exercise control over the information diet of the many without recurring to frontal censorship they simply need to heighten the volume and contradictory content of the information at the disposal of the many, wait for them to tire and become exasperated trying to figure it all out, and then present themselves as the solution to their growing sense of disorientation and exhaustion.

And sadly, many, if not most people will see their submission to the supposed mental clarity offered them by authorities not as the abject capitulation of their individual decision-making prerogative it is, but as a form of liberation. And they will attach to the authority figure's person and/or the institution he or she represents, a devotion quite similar to that which a child will offer a person they perceive as having saved them from a perilous situation.

This is the infantilizing dynamic at the center of the fact-checking industry. And as is the case in all relationships between clerics and commoners, its vigor and durability is greatly enhanced by the deployment, on the part of the clerics, of an ideal that is both highly attractive and flatly impossible to achieve.

The unicorn of unbiased news

If there is one element that is found in virtually all of the fascist movements of the 20th century it is their leaders' rhetorical pose of being above the frequently off-putting hurly-burly of politics. But, of course, no one operating in the public arena is ever above politics, or for that matter, ideology, both of which are just two more examples of the structure-engendering cultural practices alluded to above.

The same thing is true, as we have seen, in the matter of discourse which is our prime tool for turning raw information into cultural artifacts that suggest palpable meanings. As Hayden White makes clear in his masterful *Metahistory*, there is no such thing as a "virgin" approach to turning an agglomeration of facts into a coherent rendering of the past. Why? Because every writer or speaker of history is also necessarily a previous reader of it, and as such, has internalized a series of verbal conventions that are deeply freighted with ideological meanings.

He reminds us, moreover, that every act of narration undertaken by a writer involves both the suppression or foregrounding of certain facts in relation to others. So even if you provide two writers with the exact same factual materials, they will inevitably produce narratives that are different in their tone, as well as their implied semantic and ideological emphases.

We can thus say that while there are more or less careful chroniclers of the social reality (the first groups type being conscious of the above-sketched complexities and traps, while the second group are far less so) what there are not, and never will be, are fully objective or unbiased ones

Confounding the matter further is the infinitely complex set of suppositions, often rooted in collective history and personal context, that a given reader brings to the task of deciphering the already freighted choices of the chronicler, something that Terry Eagleton points out in humorous fashion in the following passage.

"Consider a prosaic, quite unambiguous statement like the one sometimes seen in the London Underground system: 'Dogs must be carried on the escalator.' This is not perhaps quite as unambiguous as it seems at first sight: does it mean that you must carry a dog on the escalator? Are you likely to be banned from the escalator unless you can find some stray mongrel to clutch in your arms on the way up? Many apparently straightforward notices contain such ambiguities: 'Refuse to be put in this basket,' for instance, or the British road-sign 'Way Out' as read by a Californian."

When we take the time to think about it, we can see that human communication is extremely complicated, necessarily ambiguous, and full of misunderstandings. It is, as is often said about baseball, "a game of percentages" in which what we say, or our interlocutor heard, will often differ greatly from the concept or idea that might have seemed crystal clear in our minds before we opened our mouths and tried to share it with that person.

This inherently "relational," and therefore slippery nature of language, and hence the impossibility of expressing absolute, immutable or wholly objective truths through any of its modalities has been widely understood since the promulgation of Saussure's linguistic theories in the early years of the 20th century, and needless to say, in a less abstract manner for thousands of years before that.

But now our "fact-checkers" are telling us that this is not the case, that there is such a thing as fully objective news that exists above the din of necessarily partial and gaffe-laden human dialogues, and surprise, surprise, they just happen to possess it.

This is, in the very real genealogical sense, a fascist trick if there ever was one.

As much as they liked to suggest it, Mussolini, Franco, Salazar and Hitler were never above politics or ideology. And our fact-checkers are not, and never will be above linguistic and therefore, conceptual imprecision and semantic shading.

Why? Because no one or no institution ever is above politics. And anyone who tells or suggests that they are or can be is—no need beating around the bush—an authoritarian who either does not understand the mechanics of human freedom and democracy, or does, and is quite intentionally trying to destroy them.

21 March 2022

THE BRUTAL POLITICS OF BRANDING

O ver the summer, I received an email from "your" Faculty Secretary—as she sometimes refers to herself in notes to her colleagues—inviting me to participate in the branding sessions being run by a consultant recently hired by the college.

So, it has finally come to this, I thought. We, a group of extravagantly trained thinkers have given up the pretense that rigorously honed ideas and arguments matter, and have finally surrendered to the logic of "liquid modernity," a space wherein the fabrication of would-be images and momentary sensations regularly trump the joys and lessons of primary experience.

I am not naive about the often calculated and calculating reality of self-presentation, nor the enormous role it has played in human affairs throughout history. There has been, and always will be, a gap in what we believe ourselves to more or less be in essence and the various faces we present to the world.

What is troubling today is how the balance in this ever-present dichotomy now seems to lean inordinately toward the arts of imposture, and a situation in which the always tensed cords linking the essential and the portrayable elements of life have begun to snap.

Not too long ago, the cultivation of a wholesale disjunction between one's inner thoughts and outer presentation was broadly seen as pathological. Now, however, the ability to propagate free-floating images of the self (and with it one's chosen causes) is now presented as proof of good sense and high intelligence.

Just think about the millions of young people who now spend infinitely more time curating their online personas than actually finding out who they are and what they believe in through face-to-face dialogue.

Branding is derived from the middle English term to "impress or burn a mark upon with a hot iron, to cauterize, to stigmatize" a practice with clearly painful and violative intent when visited, as it frequently was in the past, on fellow human beings.

When we cauterize human flesh we are, in effect, canceling its relationship to the rest of the organism of which it forms a part, setting in motion a process that mocks the promise of the redeeming "true symbol" which, according to Joseph Campbell, is "always a token that restores, one way or another, some kind of broken unit."

What do we lose when this disjunction between parts and wholes becomes normalized in a culture, when our minds are constantly being "seared" by unidimensional representations of inherently complex realities? It would seem to be a question worth exploring.

While political branding has always been with us, it appears to have taken a quantum leap in audacity and intensity in the first decade of the 21st century. First came the massive "with us or against us" propaganda campaign in favor of the destruction of Iraq.

Then came the Obama campaign for the presidency, wherein the long-standing tradition of flogging an attractive set of images while limiting the issuance of concrete policy commitments, gave way to the practice of concentrating almost exclusively on the former at the expense of the latter.

Back then, I remember having conversation after conversation with well-educated Democratic voters confident that Obama was going to be a wonderful progressive president, people who, when pressed, generally could not point to any concrete policy proposals that led them to this conclusion.

And when it was pointed out to them that he had made a number of moves in his pre-political career and his brief time in the Senate that marked him as a rather reliable supporter of traditional and generally quite conservative centers of financial and military power, most would not hear of it.

And the minority that would engage with such challenges were quick to explain, in the absence of any documented proof that if he was saying and doing these counterintuitive things, it was to get elected, and that all would change for the progressive good when he finally got into office.

Simply a case of a war-fatigued electorate getting ahead of itself? That no doubt was a factor.

But given what we now know about the important role that the well-known advocate for government-administered nudges, Cass Sunstein, played in the Obama administration, the nearly seamless partnership that the 44th President would enjoy with spymaster and serial scenographer of psychological operations John Brennan, and the outsized role that behavioral insight teams now play at all administrative levels of our society, it seems licit to ask if something much more planned and systematic might have been taking place.

When we take the time to listen carefully to those closest to power (who in my limited experience with them often have an uncanny way of betraying their true ideas and intentions) it becomes clear that they have been thinking about how to promote these patterns of cognitive decoupling in the general population for a long time.

When, as I serially remind people, Karl Rove told journalist Ron Suskind about the Bush Administration's ability to create its "own realities"— virtual facts that would always outpace the ability of the journalists and others in what he called the "reality-based community" to deactivate them in the minds of the public—he was copping to doing precisely this.

Rahm Emanuel demonstrated a similar candor in 2010 when asked to comment on the growing liberal discontent with President Obama's large-scale abandonment of progressive policy positions when he said: "They like the president, and that's all that counts," by which it seems he really meant something like this.

"We have invested a lot of time and money in creating an image of the president that appeals to virtue-seeking liberals. Our polling tells us that when forced to choose between that carefully constructed image of Obama and what their lying eyes are telling them about the true nature of his policies, most will choose the former."

It seems increasingly obvious that our political operatives, and the Deep State/Corporate coalition for whom they mostly work, now trust quite deeply in their ability to use branding to induce what social psychologist Albert Bandura describes as the selective activation and deactivation of the public's moral instincts.

Bandura finds the second outcome, which he terms "moral disengagement" to be especially troubling as it can open the door to the widespread dehumanization of those who refuse to abandon their personal agency in the midst of the pressure to conform to the particular, usually elite-inspired, groupthink of the moment.

Here, according to Bandura are some of the hallmarks of the phenomenon.

"The moral disengagement may center on the cognitive restructuring of inhumane conduct into a benign or worthy one by moral justification, sanitizing language, and advantageous comparison; disavowal of a sense of personal agency by diffusion or displacement of responsibility; disregarding or minimizing the injurious effects of one's actions; and attribution of blame to, and dehumanization of those who are victimized. Many inhumanities operate through a supportive network of legitimate enterprises run by otherwise considerate people who contribute to destructive activities by disconnected subdivision of functions and diffusion of responsibility. Given the many mechanisms for disengaging moral control, civilized life requires, in addition to humane personal standards, safeguards built into social systems that uphold compassionate behavior and renounce cruelty".

Could there be a better description of the comportment over the last two years of the overwhelmingly "liberal" and well-credentialed group of Covid maximalists in our midst?

Yes, it was the Bush administration, working off what it learned about media management from the Panama invasion and Gulf War I, that first put Karl Rove's reality creation machine into full gear.

But it has been the so-called progressives who have brought the politics of branding—with its open assaults on those calling for integrative analysis and problem-solving—to new heights, first through its cover-the-eyes denial of Obama's abject corporatism and war-mongering, then through its fact-free pursuit of the Russiagate scandal and now, most consequentially perhaps, with its consistently reality-denying approach to Covid.

Here we have a population cohort, whose sense of social and political identity is very much bound up in the idea that they are more far-seeing and more moral than those they oppose in social debates, blithely signing off on mass house arrests, the surefire inducement of cognitive and developmental delays in millions of children and, most gravely, the flat-out abrogation of the concept of bodily sovereignty. And all in the absence of solid empirical evidence for the efficacy of the policies they have imposed and/or endorsed.

It is not hyperbole to say that 20-30 percent of the US population, comprising a healthy percentage of its most highly credentialed citizens, live in a perpetual fugue state wherein following directives from "properly branded" intellectual authorities, and reflexively ridiculing those that the same authorities cursorily signal as aberrant, is now the norm. This mental pattern consistently overwhelms any desire on their part to engage in an autonomous review of available data.

The Example of Spain

This is not the first time that an imperial elite, obsessed with the iconography of its own omnipotence has mentally closed in upon itself in this way.

In the middle of the 16th century Spain's political, economic and cultural power was immense, and in many ways comparable to that of the US in the half century or so following World War II. Nothing taking place in an arc that went from Chile to Vienna passing through Peru, Colombia, Mexico, the Caribbean, the Low Countries, much of central Europe, and most of the Italian Peninsula was immune to its power.

The Vatican, which was still the center of religious life for most of the citizens in these places, never undertook any major campaign or change without first considering how it would be viewed at the Escorial, the built-to-impress seat of Spanish kings outside of Madrid.

And yet, at the end of the first quarter of the 17th century, it was clear the Spanish moment had passed. Yes, there were—it is worth noting—expensive and ill-chosen wars and disastrous economic policies that shunned domestic investment in favor of what we would today call outsourcing to foreign manufacturers and payments to foreign creditors. But perhaps more importantly, there was the generalized failure of the country's elites to recognize and adapt to the changing realities of the world.

As England and the Low Countries forged ahead in the development of the scientific method and the principles of modern capitalism, thereby creating an imperative for a rearrangement of the European concert of nations, Spain first scoffed at their new approaches and then sought to put them back in their rightful places though expensive and wasteful wars.

What Spain's elites, with a few exceptions, seldom if ever did was to stop and ask hard questions about the precepts under which they were doing business, and what, if anything, those that were gaining on them were doing that might be worth imitating. On the contrary, they tended to enact ever more strict censorship and orchestrated campaigns of disdain for foreigners and their ideas.

The rest of the story is not pretty and revolves during the next three centuries or so around progressive impoverishment, repeated civil wars and a retreat into the status of a cultural and political backwater.

And yet so great was their continuing hubris and delusional belief in Spain's status as one of the great poles of world culture in the 1950s and 1960s that the country's dictatorial bureaucrats proudly banned books by seminal thinkers and unashamedly and unironically referred to the country as the "Sentinel of Western Culture."

Will this be our fate?

For the sake of my children, I certainly hope not.

If we are to avoid it, we must remind ourselves of Campbell's idea of "true symbols" and how, above all, they help us repair what has been broken. While we must always frontally rebut the falsehoods that the brand-conscious idea-makers rain down upon us, we cannot and should not allow ourselves to get too caught up in the vortex of their self-referential fantasies about self and others.

To do so would be to take energy away from our prime of job of engendering psychological and spiritual repair which, as thinkers like Matthew Crawford and Sinead Murphy have recently argued, can only come from forging sturdy associative bonds.

Bonds created, not on the basis of top-down directives, but rather from a frank estimation of our individual states of fragility, and our knowledge that the only thing that has ever saved us from that state of being are good-faith, eye-to-eye meetings across dinner tables, work-benches, scrapbooking groups, or wherever else people gather in the hope of connecting, building or renewing something together.

23 March 2022

A HELPLESS, WEARY AND
TRAUMATIZED POPULACE

W hen most people hear the terms "shock and awe" and "full spectrum dominance" they probably think—if they think about them at all—of the early moments of the premeditated US destruction of Iraq and the ever-smug grin of Donald Rumsfeld.

It was Rumsfeld, you will recall, who supposedly spent the first months of his mandate as Secretary of Defense totally rethinking the mechanics of the US way of making war.

At the center of the new defense doctrine were the two approaches mentioned above.

The first refers to the practice of hitting the enemy so hard, so quickly, and from so many angles that he will immediately recognize the futility of mounting a defense and rapidly give up the struggle.

The second tactic, which is subsumed by the first, refers, among other things, to the practice of inundating the informational environments of the enemy, the domestic US audience and potential US allies with pro-American narratives that leave absolutely no space or time for formulating skeptical questions or coherent discourses of dissent.

In short, the overarching goal of Rumsfeld's new defense doctrine was—to use a term near and dear to the hearts of James Mitchell and Bruce Jessen who earned millions from the US Defense department after September 11th for designing the torture programs used at Guantanamo Bay and other US black sites around the world—to induce "learned helplessness" in as many segments of the world population as was technically possible.

For many, I think, the idea that governments might have the capacity and the desire to assault their own populations with well-organized and persistent campaigns of information warfare seems rather far-fetched.

And for others, I suspect, speaking of the widespread infliction of "trauma" in this context might evoke comparisons to some of the worst forms of whiny and exaggerated campus wokery.

But after all we have seen over the last several decades of world history, is the idea that governments might often be strategically motivated, serial abusers of their own populations really so hard to acknowledge?

We know, as I have previously mentioned, that when the US-backed Italian government was faced with the growing possibility of having to share power with that country's Communist Party in the 1970s and 1980s, elements of the government or close to it greenlighted a number of false flag attacks on the Italian police and the general population, the most notable of these being the Bologna train station massacre of 1980.

The aim of the attacks, as was subsequently explained by one of the government-protected terrorists, Vicenzo Vinciguerra, was to generate a social panic that would drive those disaffected with the country's social and economic reality back into the arms of the increasingly discredited, but US-approved Christian-Democrat party.

It was his witness of these events as an anti-establishment activist that impelled the philosopher Giorgio Agamben to write his influential studies on the architectures of social control used by contemporary Western governments, studies that suggest among many other things, that generating "states of exception" wherein the normal deliberative processes of the society are suspended or gravely curtailed, has become standard operating procedure in many Western "democracies."

I think few would now dispute that, whatever the origins of the attacks of September 11th, the widespread sense of trauma generated within the US population by the repetitive broadcasting of that day's horrific images greatly facilitated the government's drive to radically redefine longstanding notions of civil liberty and achieve citizen buy-in for its multiple wars of aggression in the Middle East.

All of which bring us to Covid.

Can anyone who has read Laura Doddsworth's essential *A State of Fear*, or read the German government's so-called "Panic Paper" really doubt the conscious and cynical desire by governments, who supposedly serve at the pleasure of the people, to inflict trauma on the general populations of those countries?

Does a German government that is not interested in heightening tensions and leveraging them to achieve greater compliance to official edicts among the population propose in a planning document that its officials a) concentrate only on worst case Covid scenarios, b) explicitly eschew the need to model the economic effects of proposed mitigation strategies c) downplay the fact that the disease kills mostly very old people d) endeavor to produce "the desired shock effect" and induce guilt in children about possibly being the catalyst in the death of their older relatives?

Yes, people all across the Western world and beyond were purposely traumatized by the very people who never ceased telling them that their only true concern was to "keep them safe."

While I am not a psychologist, this much I know. The enormously disorienting and cognitively debilitating effects of trauma are fed, more than anything else, by the maintenance of a fundamentally reactive posture in relation to the world around us. The trauma is greatly diminished when we stop, breathe and, to the best of our ability, fearlessly catalog the injuries we have suffered, ask who authored them, and, if relevant, what made so many of us acquiescent to these assaults upon our dignity and well-being.

People at the highest levels of Government, Hi-tech, Big Capital and Big Pharma are keenly aware of what I just said, and thus will do all in their power to keep us de-centered and highly attentive to the ever-changing and mostly trivial info-bites they constantly send our way.

While for us calm and catharsis are the first steps to regaining our integrity, for them they are kryptonite.

So far, it seems, these large centers of power are winning the struggle. Here in the US, as well as the countries in Europe I have recently visited, most citizens seem to have contented themselves, as the serially abused often do, with the temporary cessation of assaults against their dignity and inherent social rights. Few, it seems, are ready to look into the recent past with any sustained passion or vigor.

I wish I knew what might help some of these people recognize the state of learned helplessness into which they have fallen, and how to spur in them the process of spiritual and civic reconstruction in themselves and others. However, I don't.

And perhaps it's hubristic of me to think that I might have this capability in the first place.

When in doubt or seemingly stuck in place, I was once told, the first step is seeking out those whose inner lights seem to be burning most brightly, and offering to walk beside them in hope.

Right now, perhaps that's the best we can all do.

4 June 2022

THE MILGRAM EXPERIMENT RESTAGED, THIS TIME WITH MILLIONS OF REAL VICTIMS

Pretty much everyone out there has some familiarity with the Milgram experiment, the study conducted at Yale University in 1961 under the direction of psychology professor Stanley Milgram. The idea of the experiment was to test the extent to which people would be inclined to dispense with whatever moral scruples or empathic instincts they have when asked by an authority figure to inflict pain on innocent people.

To the surprise of many, well over half of the of the individuals (termed "teachers" in the experiment) tasked with enforcing the torturous will of the authority figure (termed "the experimenter") on the third-party participants (termed "students") in the experiment did so with brio and little apparent consternation.

All of the victims ("students") in the experiment were actors. Even with this being so, a seeming plurality of contemporary scholars have concluded that the professor's *mise-en-scène* was unethical because he violated the prohibition against the use of deception in experiments with human subjects when he made the "teachers" believe they were actually meting out pain to the students.

You've got to love the ever small-bore nature academic minds, don't you?

They are able to endlessly parse the possible deleterious effects of experiments on human subjects when serving on college Institutional Review Boards (IRBs), and can engage in spirited debates about the ethics of one of the world's most famous and telling psychological experiments more than fifty years after the fact.

But when it comes to using their exquisite training to look at what is, by far, the largest experiment on human subjects in history (the lockdowns and vaccine mandates)—one that clearly violates the core ethical tenets of informed consent and medical necessity, not to mention the US laws governing the administration of EUA products and the EEOC guidelines on the use of coercive incentives to achieve vaccine uptake—they mostly have nothing to say.

But even more troubling, if that is possible, is their widespread failure to recognize and harshly condemn what has been, in effect, the staging of a massive new version of the Milgram experiment in our time, wherein government officials, the media and medical experts actively and quite blithely encourage the infliction of pain upon those citizens who were simply uncomfortable with being forced to take highly experimental drugs with no proven track record or safety history.

Got a family member who actually did some homework on the injections, and knew they were never expected to protect against transmission? No, problem, ban him from Thanksgiving and all other family gatherings and suggest to others behind his back that he's gone off the deep end.

Got a previously-infected colleague with enough intellectual confidence to do her own research about the concept of natural immunity, and thus see through the transparent lies spread by government agencies about the quality and duration of that protection against infection and serious illness? No problem, label her an ignorant anti-vaxxer and cheer your bosses as they show her the door for non-compliance. This, even though she is, Covid-wise, probably the safest person to be near in the workplace.

Know someone who actually read the large corpus of studies showing the rank ineffectiveness of masks as a mitigation measure amongst the general public and who, in the hopes of stimulating a productive discussion posted links to many of them on the company communication channels? No problem, hoot him down *en masse* and suggest quite clearly to him that if he knows what's good for himself, he'll never do anything like that again.

I could go on.

The list of ways Milgram-like "teachers" – people who voluntarily supported the drive to inflict social and financial pain upon those with the temerity to maintain their intellectual and moral integrity in the face of a clearly manufactured crisis – is nearly infinite.

But looking around and listening to people today, it's as if none of it ever happened. No significant apologies have been issued by anyone in charge. And worse yet, perhaps, no one in the family and friendship circles I know of has acknowledged what they did or supported others to do in the way of inflicting pain.

No one of any consequence has acknowledged, never mind apologized for the injustice done to the *millions of people*—I'll say that again *millions of people*—who lost their livelihoods for their refusal to take an experimental drug whose performance has completely betrayed all the "do-it-because-we're-all-in-this-together" arguments that were bullyingly deployed on its behalf.

Have any of the people who made this possible either as policy-makers or as corporate pain-enforcers spearheaded a move to repair the enormous damage they have inflicted on individuals and families, many of whom find themselves in financial and psychological holes from which they will never emerge?

These Milgramite "experimenters" and "teachers" knew exactly what they were doing. Indeed, many of them, like our President, clearly relished initiating and firing up a "stick-it-to-your-fellow-citizen" movement among us.

Now, however, we're all supposed to forget about that, because, as everyone in polite, credentialed company knows, the open expression of anger is, as you know darling, just so *déclassé* and just so, um, unseemly.

Maybe so. And it's true that our social elites have done an awfully good job over the last forty years of making people feel ashamed of harboring essential human emotion.

But some of us, many more than I think they realize, have continued to give ourselves permission to access this protean force, this emotional superfood, which has always played a key role in the pursuit of justice.

And we, as the Dixie Chicks sang, are "Not ready to make nice" and "not ready to back down."

STIGMATIZE, SURROUND, AND STOMP

This past week the Tampa Bay Rays staged a Pride Night designed, as the club's president Matt Silverman said, to show that at "our games that the LGBTQ+ community is invited, welcomed and celebrated." And as part of the event, they asked the team's players to wear specially designed LGBTQ+ rainbow hats during the game.

Nice touch. Right? After all, who could be against the idea of affirming people's right to do whatever they want with their bodies and to develop a lifestyle in consonance with those urges? Certainly not me.

But what if it's not that simple? What if the standard reasoning for staging such events—to promote tolerance and a respect for difference—has a darker side that no one really wants to talk about, and that very much feeds into encouraging the enormous breaches of civility that we have witnessed in our culture over the past two plus years?

When it comes to judging electoral systems, one of the key indicators of their health is the degree to which citizens are guaranteed privacy when casting their votes. The reason is clear. Privacy and anonymity in voting ensure that individual citizens can't be singled out and punished by those presently in power who just might not like the political program they have chosen to endorse with their votes.

The guarantee of a secret ballot also speaks to a broader if at times less explicitly articulated democratic principle: that there is, and should always be a clear barrier between the private and public spheres of our lives.

Put another way, no one whom I have not voluntarily invited into my inner circle of trust should have the right to cast judgment upon me for the things I read, or the speculations I conjure while sitting in my easy chair at home.

The only thing that should be a licit target for the praise or reproach of others is my legal and moral comportment in the public square.

This is why it is considered taboo, when not patently illegal, to ask certain personal questions during job interviews.

But what happens when a powerful entity with the ability to heavily condition the lives of citizens embraces clearly ideological constructs, like say, the positive celebration of LGBTQ+ rights, or the essential infallibility of CDC guidance in public health matters, as its official policy?

On first inspection, it would seem there is nothing to worry about. After all, what organization does not implicitly embrace some ideological posture or another?

The problem comes when the people who have power in the organization *openly demand a public affirmation of the chosen ideological construct*, or more diabolically, set up a situation wherein the employee or citizen is forced to choose between violating their conscience (by publicly professing an adherence belief to which they do not subscribe) or outing themselves as a dissident to company policy, with all that that implies in terms of inviting possible reprisals from the power holders.

This is, in effect, what was done in almost all the totalitarian dictatorships of the last century.

And this is what the Tampa Bay Rays did to their players the other night by asking that they make a symbolic statement in favor of a political and ideological construct that has no clear relationship to the job they were hired to do.

As it turns out, five of the players on the team refused to do so, on the basis, it appears, of their religious beliefs. They have been widely criticized for doing so, with the *NYT* saying their actions "undercut" the ideological celebration planned by the ownership.

Get it?

Freedom of conscience is out. The real responsibility of the players, according to the Gray Lady, was to seamlessly parrot the wholly extraneous ideological line of their employer whether they believed in it or not.

The truth is they should have never, ever, been put in that position.

This, just as no one on a job interview or performance review should ever be asked about the details of their religious observance, their particular political activities, or what they do in their bedroom with self or other.

The trend toward this brand of "coerced solidarity" carries with it the additional problem of suggesting to the citizenry that what we say or express symbolically is more important than what we do.

I don't know how the five players have treated the LGBTQ+ people with whom they've crossed paths in life. And neither, I suspect, do any of the people who are now criticizing them for their failure to publicly identify with the team's chosen ideological program.

While it might be striking news for the many young people who have come of age in the era of online media mobbing, it's perfectly possible for people to have a strong moral conviction about something and treat people who in their mind violate it with kindness, courtesy and even friendship. It is also possible for a person of a particular ideological persuasion who flaunts all the right symbols to treat someone who shares their belief system and issues all the right words and symbols used to affirm it, quite abominably.

Why did the management of the Tampa Bay Rays seemingly feel perfectly empowered to impose a public loyalty test—one that would have been unthinkable as recently as a few years ago—upon their employees?

Because for the last two plus years they have watched their own government, working in conjunction with a wholly co-opted media do precisely this to the US citizenry.

Official ideological positions; that is, positions that are presented as unquestioningly good for all and thus above debate now regularly emanate from our government and have their effectively transcendent status vigorously defended by the media. The process looks something like this.

1. First comes a policy which, as I have said, is described by the government and its media handmaidens as being resolutely for the common good, and as such, beyond any reasoned debate regarding its advisability and efficacy.
2. A talisman is developed and deployed (a useless mask, a vaccine card) to serve as a visible marker of the citizen's conformity to the supposedly wholly beneficent and thus fundamentally

undebatable ideological program.

3. As expected, a minority of the society questions whether the project in question is as immaculately conceived and wholly altruistic as they are being told. And they often express their discontent by eschewing the implied demand to sport the government's talisman of ideological conformity.

4. In so doing, they effectively "out" themselves as "problematic" before their more pliant fellow citizens.

5. This delights the cynical elites who have set the whole festival of officialist virtue signaling in motion, as it provides them with a readily identifiable symbol of hate-worthiness, a vast field of humanoid bloody socks if you will, with which to further inflame the passions of the great mass of conformists.

6. Seeing the very real possibility that they too might be subject to a moral lynching, other nonconformists will naturally think twice about violating the verbal and semiotic codes of compliance in the future.

7. The officialist ideology thus takes on an appearance of popularity that it does not in fact have in reality which, in turn, further convinces other possible nonconformists of the futility of seeking to resist it.

8. Lather, rinse and repeat.

Where to go from here? I'm not exactly sure. However, I think I know of a couple of good places to start.

The first is to remind people again and again that in a halfway functioning democracy *nothing is ever beyond debate* for the simple reason that no one or no corporate entity, no matter how powerful they may appear, has a monopoly on wisdom, truth, or morality.

The second is to revive a simple practice that was known to, and modeled by, all the adults in my extended family when I was a kid, but that seems to have been largely forgotten under the pressures of an online culture that assumes the information from our inner lives is there to be plundered for profit of others.

What is it?

When someone asks you to share something that is not theirs to know, and could be used by unscrupulous others to defame or control you, you look them straight in the eye and exclaim in sharp tones and without the slightest hint of a smile: "It's none of your damn business."

13 June 2022

BILL GATES AND THE FRAME GAME

A few weeks back, at the World Economic Forum (WEF) meeting in Davos, Bill Gates said some surprising things. In the course of a 56-minute panel discussion the vaccine pusher extraordinaire admitted (starting at the 18:22 mark) that the Covid vaccines do not block infection and that the duration of whatever protection they bring to the table is extremely short.

He later talked (starting at the 51:00 mark) of the absurdity of implementing any Covid passport program—and one can logically deduce any other measure to segregate the vaccinated from the unvaccinated—when the injections have shown no ability to do the least that one should expect from a vaccine: prevent infection and transmission.

These admissions violently kick the stool out from under the arguments made in favor of vaccine mandates, many of which are still being pursued with pitiless vigor by public officials, CEOs, and educational administrators all around the world.

Are we to believe that Bill Gates had a sudden impulse to undermine all that he used his billions to mercilessly promote over the last two years? And that he was giving all those currently carrying out those plans permission to stand down?

It's a nice thought. But I don't believe it to be the case.

No. Bill was simply engaging in one of the more tried and true techniques of elite information management, the limited hangout, or what I prefer to call a drive to "save the frame" of an argument that is quickly losing its coherence.

Since Bill and many of the people he has paired up with to force the experimental and often harmful vaccines upon the world effectively own or have donated untold amounts of money to many of the world's more important media outlets, he knew beforehand that he did not have to worry much about his words being widely circulated.

And so it was. Only relatively small independent news gatherers took any note of what he said.

So who was he addressing his words to and why?

He was speaking to the fellow true believers and providing them with a rhetorical model for handling the loss of faith some in their ranks are having in the face of the vaccines' abject failure.

The key to understanding the frame game here is the clause Gates uttered right before the "but" with which he introduced his truthful words about the "vaccines" pitiful infection-blocking capabilities and short duration of effectiveness: "The vaccines have saved millions of lives."

Those familiar with the work of cognitive linguist George Lakoff, or the activities of pollster and political wordsmith Frank Luntz will know what I'm talking about.

What these two men have in common—despite their divergent political allegiances—is their belief in the extraordinary power of rhetorical framing; that is, the tendency of the human brain to subordinate the careful analysis of empirically proven details to the embrace of an overarching cognitive metaphor that appeals to their deeper, if often unstated, cultural and emotional values.

It's the difference, for example, between "The US invaded Iraq on false pretenses and destroyed it, killing hundreds of thousands of innocent people," and "In its efforts to bring democracy to Iraq, the US made a number of tragic mistakes."

The first states a bald empirical truth. The second obfuscates that crude reality and subordinates it to the noble vision, so cherished by Americans when contemplating their role in the world, of a country that is constantly helping people around the world to better their lives.

With the widespread distribution of mental frames like this in the media, "poof!" go all the gory, on-the-ground details, and with them more importantly, the need to actually interrogate what we did and how we might seek to repair the lives we broke.

Going back to Davos, Bill was effectively saying to his minions, "You are on a great moral crusade. We've had some small problems along the way, but don't give up, because the world needs us to continue to be heroic and save more lives."

And with that cognitive frame in place, any creeping doubts those in the audience might have about what they have done, and their future mission, disappear just like that.

We see the same gambit used when the US government inevitably links the apparent waning of the pandemic to the use of vaccines. Here, for example, is what the CDC said to CNN shortly after lifting requirement that US citizens be tested before returning home from foreign travels:

"The Covid-19 pandemic has now shifted to a new phase, due to the widespread uptake of highly effective Covid-19 vaccines, the availability of effective therapeutics, and the accrual of high rates of vaccine-and infection-induced immunity at the population level in the United States. Each of these measures has contributed to lower risk of severe disease and death across the United States."

It's no accident that the first factor adduced to explain the onset of happier days, the one that sets the frame for all that follows, is the "widespread uptake of highly effective Covid-19 vaccines."

The goal here—as it was in the case of Gates at Davos—is to preserve, in the face of abundant empirical evidence to the contrary, the frame that presents the forced administration of vaccines as the great slayer of the pandemic and gifter of our vanquished freedoms, and to turn that suggestion into an established fact through constant repetition.

But, of course, neither Gates's claim about the vaccines saving "millions of lives" nor the CDCs' assertion that "widespread vaccine uptake" was the key reason for ending the pandemic are established facts. Far from it. Indeed, there are no scientific studies that l know of capable of authenticating either claim. But that's just the point.

The elites that deign to rob us of our bodily sovereignty and so much more in the name of Covid, or whatever other "mortal health threat" that they choose to publicize next through their carpet-bomber control of most media, have all done their homework on the frame game and carefully tailor their communications to fit within its imperatives.

Unfortunately, most citizens are still not clued in to how it operates in their lives. Verbal details such as the ones cited above matter because they play an enormous role in establishing and maintaining what the now sadly tarnished Chomsky once brilliantly called the field of "thinkable thought" in our public discussions.

To open up that field we need to smash *their* frames. But to smash those frames we first need to admit they exist.

6 June 2022

THE ERIC ADAMS CURE FOR NON-COMPLIANCE: COMPLIANCE

As everyone knows, there is a public employee shortage that, *of course*, has nothing to do with vaccine mandates. This is true, just as every thinking person knows that there are nursing shortages, pilot shortages, and clear upticks in sudden deaths among world-class athletes, soldiers and ordinary people between 17 and 49 that, *of course,* also have nothing to do with vaccine mandates.

Because he's a smart guy who peruses the *New York Times* each morning and follows the science, New York mayor Eric Adams knows this as well.

And this is why he has just reached out to the many of the misguided people who walked away from their city jobs over the requirement to take experimental, almost wholly useless, and often quite dangerous injections with an offer they can't refuse.

They can have their jobs back and all will be forgiven if they ...are you ready for the big sweetener? ...they just get the jab.

Amnesty! Such a deal!

The kindly and witty letter he sent to some of them (which I have seen) underscored the self-evident line of continuity between achieving good health and doing what you're told by the government: "In order to *cure your non-compliance* you must submit proof of vaccination to the Employee Health Program."

Sarcasm aside, the mayor's vaccine amnesty "solution" is quite instructive as it lays bare the cognitive patterns that predominate in those who deem themselves to be on the cutting edge of thinking and governance in our culture today.

The first thing it shows is their aggressive ignorance. For all their talk about following the science, they'd rather be tortured at Guantanamo Bay than actually read it. Given that the vaccines do not prevent infection or transmission there is absolutely no social reason to get the vaccine and thus no reason to compel anyone to take it. Period.

And because these self-styled cultural and political leaders have done everything in their power to not get informed as serious people do when facing crucial life questions, they honestly believe there is nothing to discuss.

And people who truly believe that there is nothing to discuss and argue about when it comes to implementing massively impactful policies touching several aspects of our social contract and our social fabric are, *per se*, acting in a highly authoritarian fashion.

They also seem to think that most people are truly dumb. In the particular case of Adams, for example, he seems to presume that they do not know that he has waived city vaccine requirements for mostly wealthy professional athletes and entertainers, and that humble ex-municipal employees can't perceive this flagrant double-standard.

But perhaps more important and telling than all of this in the long run is Adams and company's pathetic understanding of human psychology, especially the central role that belief, moral convictions, and the search for dignity still play in the lives of millions of people.

These self-appointed bringers of the new and *of course* infinitely more just and healthy new world to come are convinced, as the full-bore creatures of a materially-bound consumerist thinking that they are, that everyone else also views the world in strictly transactional terms.

Sure, they admit, some of the resistant people do often adduce historically-anchored moral arguments for not accepting the wonderful gifts they and their fellow vanguards are selflessly offering them.

But as these same vanguards know all too well from their successful experiences of climbing up the institutional ladder, most, if not all, moral arguments deployed today are pretextual, mere smokescreens for tactically obscuring the presence of the amoral self-seeker that they know ultimately governs every person's comportment in the world.

"Did any of us actually believe any of that save-the-world twaddle the admissions consultants our parents hired told us to put on our college application essays?" they ask themselves.

"Of course not!" comes back the resounding response.

And so it is, they conclude, for the non-compliant.

In this context then, the key as they see it is to just look past all the verbal and gestural bluster and determine resistors' real price because, as they know, everybody has a price.

It's just a matter of finding it.

And the most effective methods toward achieving this end—as the US foreign policy establishment has been modeling to our domestic elites for decades—are concerted campaigns of insults and the pointed infliction of financial pain. No arguments or sweeteners are ever needed.

Dignity? Transcendent values? Redemptive suffering?

Eric Adams and his friends know that's just desperate verbal filler deployed by eternal losers who, incongruously, have no desire to be "cured" of the childish "illness" of non-compliance before the reality of brute force.

There you have it. Transactionalist "wisdom" at its zenith.

25 June 2022

THE SOMETIME REWARDS OF
BEING SUCKERED

"Sucker!" In early adolescence there are few epithets that cut as deeply into one's sense of self-worth as this one. At a time when you are desperately trying to figure out how the world really works, having this word hurled your way is a stark reminder that you are still pretty clueless, and thus not up to the fundamental adult task of protecting your best interests from predatory practices.

But not everything that is cruel and hurtful is without value. Knowing you've been had can be an opportunity for reflection.

I'll go even further.

To not reflect rigorously upon the ways in which others fooled you for their own ends in the past is to remain in a state of perpetual immaturity wherein you cede much of your own agency to people who—however nice or authoritative they might seem or even be—cannot ever respond to your particular needs anywhere near as well as can a truly mindful version of yourself.

And yet most everywhere I look—at least in the relatively prosperous subculture I am lucky enough to inhabit—I see Covid suckers, suckers who, moreover, exhibit little or no curiosity about how they've been duped. Indeed, many seem to exhibit a rather tender veneration toward those who have defrauded them.

For example, while having lunch at a Chinese restaurant yesterday, I overheard a conversation at a nearby table between six mature and self-evidently well-educated people in which each and every one complained with great exasperation about how they had done everything right when it came to masks, social distancing and vaccinations and still got Covid.

But no sooner had this round-robin of complaints ended than they began talking about the urgent need to get further boosted against the deadly plague.

Question the policies? Or the efficacy of the vaccines? Call into question the quality of the information they had been provided about the virus and the vaccines? Nope. Just double and triple down on more of the same. And get suckered again.

I have to admit that my first reaction when I hear and see people acting like this is to write off the whole bunch of them as ignorant clowns. And who knows, maybe that is, in the end, the only practical solution.

But even if I do banish them from my precinct of concern, an intellectual problem remains. Why have so many otherwise high-functioning adult people been such suckers for the lies issued by the government-corporate behemoth over the last two-and-a-half years?

The reasons are many. But I think all of them are conjoined by a central cultural condition or problem: their growing incapacity for generating a sensorial and social understanding of the world around them.

We are animals, and like other animal species, we are gifted at birth with an enormous storehouse of accumulated sociobiological knowledge. True, some of it is of little application in the modern world. Much of it, however, remains incredibly useful when it comes to enhancing our chances of living relatively contented and existentially successful lives.

Perhaps the most central of these instinctual skills is learning to carefully size up the moral and intellectual reliability of people around us.

Did you ever watch dogs check each other out when passing on the sidewalk? Humans have long done the same thing. What starts as an instinct in our case is gradually honed through the careful observations that only extended and repeated social contact—in places such as the dinner table, the school lunch room or the corner bar—can provide.

It is through repeated exposure to these and many sites of intense social observation that we learn how to read body language, divine the secret codes of the eyes, the enormous human capacity for insincere language and deceit (themselves survival tools in certain contexts), and on a brighter note, irony, which, by foregrounding the multiple layers of linguistic expression, greatly enhances our ability to recognize and resolve complex life problems.

Good stuff. Right?

Yes. Unless, of course, your life goals revolve around controlling others or getting them to pine for things that they do not actually need, but whose consumption will make you rich and powerful.

For such people, the continued development in the population of the social observation skills outlined briefly above is nothing short of a nightmare. And this is why they do everything in their power to cripple people's acquisition of them.

How?

Through the nonstop flood of media messaging designed to induce, both through its clearly unassimilable volume and entropic forms of delivery, personal disorientation, and from there, grave internal doubts about the skills of social discernment most were born with and have hopefully further honed along the way.

The culmination of the process from their end is the formation of a mass of individuals that possess little or no trust in its inherent powers of observation and logic, and that are thus largely dependent upon the opinions of "experts" spouting elite-amenable ideas when navigating the most basic life issues and conflicts.

If you don't believe just how far advanced this breakdown of street smarts has gone in the population, take a look sometime at the pathetically infantile level of the questions posed at Quora each day.

Viewed in this context then, do you really think it was an accident that known-to-be useless measures against spreading the SARS-CoV-2 virus centered precisely on practices (masks, social distancing, and generational segregation) that grossly inhibit children's ability to hone their aptitude for social and interpersonal discernment during the limited time window they have for such developments?

The further one goes up the educational ladder, the more severe this process of sociocultural deracination gets. For all the talk of democracy and radical social change that takes place on campus, today's universities are deeply hierarchical and often emotionally barren places where the development of individualized forms of socio-empirical intelligence is not only not supported, but openly disdained.

Readily filling the gap left by the non-pursuit of these organic and often deeply humanizing forms of knowing are highly abstract and largely unproven policy desideratum, enforced through diktats and sanctions issued by chairs, deans and provosts, or by the more important movers and shakers in one's field of professional specialization.

In a context such as this, the rhetoric of tolerance, and the paeans to the importance of free and unfettered inquiry, become mere accessories to what everyone knows, but no one will admit, is the real object of the game: the pursuit of power and/or a recognizable alignment with its known policy aims.

This ingrained schizophrenia regarding the true nature of the professional self is probably why so many academics find it nearly impossible to acknowledge, never mind apologize for, the naked rage and aggression that drive their ever-more frequent campaigns of personal destruction against others.

And it is also probably why so many physicians are so ready to sign off on treatments whose underlying science and clinical effectiveness they know little, if anything, about. Might rules. And, beyond a bit of florid rhetoric in the case of the humanities scholars, they all know this and internally embrace it.

We live in a time when powerful forces, wielding very powerful new informational weapons, seek to place a wedge between ourselves and practices which have long been essential to the search for self-knowledge, social meaning, and the ability to promote and safeguard human dignity.

The speed with which these weapons have been deployed, and have insinuated themselves into our daily lives have left many of us dazed and confused. And history shows that when social confusion is fomented in this way, people often remit their intellectual and moral sovereignty to whatever nearby force *appears* to be most powerful and in control of the situation.

And thus it has come to pass among millions of rank-and-file citizens during the last two plus years. Let's face it, these millions of people have been suckered, suckered by shameless "leaders" into giving up hard-won freedoms, their livelihoods and their bodily sovereignty.

The good news is that many of these relatively powerless millions have woken up to what has been done to them and have, it seems, pledged to never let it occur again in their lifetimes.

It would be nice to be able to say the same about those further up the educational food chain, people like teachers, lawyers, engineers, professors and doctors. But from my admittedly limited purview, I see little evidence for the existence of a large-scale move toward a catharsis among them.

One of the central, if largely unstated, presumptions of our system of government is that those who have had the privilege of learning would keep their heads clear and step into the breach created by sudden waves of social crisis.

In our time of need, however, the vast majority of these privileged people thought not about those less fortunate than themselves, or the debt they had to the society that had rendered their lives comfortable, but rather how not to run afoul of the super-powerful above them who were purposely stirring up fear and confusion in the culture.

Having succumbed to the stark logic of "Kiss-up, kick-down" in the course of their professional training, they quickly channeled their inner Machiavellis and began suckering others into potentially very harmful behaviors on the basis of lies and half-truths.

Luckily for us, however, empirical reality has a way of taking vengeance on those who construct castles in the air and force others to make effusive statements about the solidity of their non-existent foundations. We are seeing it now, as Russia reminds us that if a struggle between paper wealth and natural resources is engaged, the latter will eventually win. And so it will be with our elite fantasists and their "see-no-evil" disciples in due time.

They have suckered many people over the last two plus years, but perhaps no one quite as completely as themselves. For their less-powerful victims who have recognized their previous naivete, there is still the possibility of redemption. But for those comfortable who continue to sequester themselves in their self-constructed house of lies, the fall, when it comes, is likely to be sudden, cruel and definitive.

6 July 2022

WHY DO WE ADORE DOGS AND DESPISE PEOPLE?

t's a pretty hard trend to miss. Over the last few decades, the amount of time and emotional energy that Americans devote to their dogs has increased exponentially.

Animals that were once a pleasant and comforting adjunct to family dynamics have, it seems, been placed near the very center of many people's emotional lives.

A few weeks back, to cite just one example, the Boston Red Sox observed a moment of silence before a game to honor the passing of the dog of the team's long-time groundskeeper.

And on the few occasions in recent years when I have given students open-ended personal essay prompts in composition classes, I have received a surprisingly large number of paeans to canine house pets, personal evocations that half a generation earlier would have had as their object a beloved parent, grandparent or a particularly important mentor.

I love dogs and thus would very much like to look at this new wave of pet-loving in a purely positive light, as the result of a conscious and laudable drive on the part of our leading institutions to stem the longstanding problem of animal mistreatment. Or to see it as a simple outgrowth of a generation and a half of children raised on the exploits of canine movie heroes like Balto, Skip and Marley.

Looking out on the broader expanse of emergent cultural behaviors, however, I find this very difficult to do as the rise of the highly anthropomorphized dog seems to coincide quite closely with that of ritualized, human-on-human cruelty in our media and our broader national culture.

No sooner had my then pre-teen children finished with Disney tales of endless canine ingenuity than they began watching, over my insistent, if archly expressed objections, festivals of orchestrated humiliation on programs such as *Chopped, America's Next Top Model,* and of course, *American Idol,* each of which used the pursuit of excellence™ as a pretext for the vicious and public assaults on the dignity of spiritually needy contestants.

As social media emerged as a dominant pathway for human communication in the early 2010s, the young raised on these reality shows took the lesson that life has *always* been a pitiless choice between total victory and abject humiliation with them into the new, disembodied public square. *The Hunger Games,* released in 2012, elevated this view of human relations into the status of an unassailable social truth.

Not surprisingly, encounters with students and advisers during my office hours, which during my first two decades of university teaching revolved largely around curricular matters, veered increasingly toward stories of the indignities they and other students suffered while "partying" from Thursday through Saturday nights.

It was horrible to listen to what privileged 20-year-olds were willing to do to their "friends" in their drive to fatten their accounts of social prestige. But even worse was seeing that most of these victims of cruelty believed there was really nothing they could do to stop these assaults on their person short of crying to the Dean of Students, a solution they rightly knew would only further complicate and embitter their lives.

When I would ask in a roundabout way why, in the case of the young women, they felt the need to line up and wait to be selected for entry to a frat party on the basis of their looks or perceived level of coolness, they shrugged and said, in effect, that's the way it is. "If you want to have a social life, you need to play by the rules."

And when I very, very obliquely mentioned to some of the male complainants that there used to be rather standard verbal and even physical ways of dispatching extreme antagonists from their lives, they looked at me as if I were from outer space.

In time, the fear of being called out—for a silly question or articulating ideological positions that went against predominant and mostly woke-anchored strains of thought—became a quite palpable presence in my classes, greatly deadening the quality of our discussions.

All of which, believe it or not, brings me back to dogs.

As I've said, I love dogs. But I've never confused the interactions I have with them with those I maintain with humans, with our marvelous capacity for irony, cognitive clarity and the full-spectrum expression of tenderness, concern and care.

But what if I had seldom, if ever, felt and received these things on a consistent basis from other people? What if I had been told again and again, in small and large ways, that human relations are mostly a zero-sum competition for ever more scarce material and reputational goods?

In this context, the unconditional and always assenting loyalty of a dog might look pretty good by comparison.

Why deal with people whom you know will hurt you and with whom you are sure to have all sorts of misunderstandings when you can channel your energies toward the much more even-keeled devotion of a dog?

What, of course, gets lost in this method of coping is the development of the interpersonal skills needed for achieving full emotional maturity and for operating as a true citizen in a democratic society.

The newly-born disinformation industry is bent on telling us that truth is a product that can and should arrive to our lives fully formed, like a ripe apple on an October tree in Connecticut. The key, they would have us believe, is simply making sure we find our way to only the "best" orchard, which of course is the one to which the "best" people have given the "best" ratings online.

But, of course the ancient Greeks and most that have followed in their wake within our Western tradition knew this view of knowledge acquisition was nonsense. They knew that truths relating to complex, multifactorial phenomena seldom arrive in neat little packages and that the best we can usually do is develop approximations to their essence through spirited and earnest interpersonal dialogues.

Call me simplistic, but I believe our culture's current obsession with the allegedly "human" qualities of dogs has a lot to do with our generalized retreat from the difficulties of finding enduring comfort and wisdom—and the foundational key to both, dialogue—with the always complex humans around us.

And I believe, in turn, that this widespread retreat from what Sara

Schulman calls "normative conflict" had an awful lot to do with enabling the assaults on human dignity and freedom committed in the name of controlling Covid.

Because I love dogs, I think I can understand some of what the canine companion of the Fenway Park groundskeeper probably meant to him during the course of his arduous hours spent on the diamond. And I understand the appeal that honoring the dog might have for much of the crowd.

But if I were the director of ceremonies for the Red Sox I'd probably tend more toward a moment of silence for say, those that have died from vaccine injuries, lost their jobs over mandates, or were forced to spend their last moments on this earth alone, forcibly separated from those who, through the construction and maintenance of loving and probably also not so loving dialogues, brought true meaning into their lives.

25 July 2022

PROXY "EVIDENCE" AND THE
MANIPULATION OF HUMAN PERCEPTIONS

Every religion is true in one way or another. It is true when
understood metaphorically. But when it gets stuck to its own
metaphors, interpreting them as facts, then you are in trouble.

~ JOSEPH CAMPBELL

One of the key drivers of modernity is the belief that human beings are at their core empirically-minded creatures who, if left to develop this innate disposition to its fullest, will in time uncover and explain all of the world's many mysteries.

It is a very compelling idea, one that has no doubt greatly contributed to energizing what is sometimes referred to as the social and material march of progress.

As an epistemic system, however, it is also plagued by a grave foundational problem: the supposition that an acculturated human being can and will assess the reality around him with more or less virgin or unbiased eyes.

As José Ortega y Gasset makes clear in his masterful short essay "Heart and Head," no human being can ever do this.

"In any landscape, in any precinct where we open our eyes, the number of visible things is practically infinite, but in any given moment we can only see a very small number of them. The line of sight must fixate upon a small group of objects and deviate from the rest, effectively neglecting those other things. In other words, we cannot see one thing without ceasing to see others, without temporarily blinding ourselves to them. To see this thing means unseeing that one, in the same way that hearing one sound means unhearing others.... To see, it is not enough that there exist, on one side, our organs of sight, and on the other, the visible object situated, as always, between other equally visible things. Rather we must lead the pupil toward this object while withholding it from the others. To see, in short, it is necessary to focus. But to focus is precisely to seek something before seeing it; it is a sort of pre-see before the see. It thus seems that every vision supposes the existence of a pre-vision, which is not the product of either the pupil or the object, but rather another, pre-existing faculty charged with directing the eyes and exploring the surroundings, a thing called attention."

In other words, human perceptions in a given moment are always mediated by previous and often quite personal cognitive, vital and sensorial experiences, and as a result, can never begin to approach the levels of neutrality or breadth of focus that we humans are presumed to be capable of having as participants in the empiricist paradigm of modernity.

Ortega thus suggests that we should—while never abandoning the search for enveloping truths—always retain a consciousness of the fact that many if not most descriptions proffered to us as exemplars of reality writ large are symbolic placeholders, or proxies, for the integral reality of the phenomenon in question.

I may be wrong, but it seems that few policymakers, and more depressingly still, few physicians today ever think about the Spanish philosopher's advice about the need to constantly engage in what Pierre Bourdieu would come to call "critical reflexivity;" that is, the ability to honestly assess the inevitable shortcomings and blind spots located within the phenomenological frames governing their daily labors.

In fact, we see much the opposite: a growing tendency among both political and scientific insiders, and from there, the general public to both naively presume the panoptic nature of the scientific gaze, and to imbue self-evidently partial or even purely theoretical "proofs" with the same evidentiary weight as results obtained in much more broadly designed trials with significant real-world outcomes.

Does this sound confusing? Perhaps an example can help.

The ostensible purpose of going to college is to get educated, which is to say, to submit one's self to a series of rigorous exercises that expand the contours and capabilities of the mind.

When watching the commercial enterprise colloquially known as college sports on TV we are frequently told of the wonderfully high graduation rates achieved by certain coaches at certain universities. The announcers speak of these wonderful graduation rates to underscore the idea that the athletes you see on your screen are studying and getting educated, and thus sustaining the stated core goal of the University.

In this context, then, we could say that the graduation rate is serving as a *proxy* for the idea that a whole lot of education is taking place among the athletes at those institutions.

But is that necessarily so? Is it not equally possible that the institution, aware of the enormous financial benefits that a powerful athletic team can bring to it, might set up graduation processes for athletes that only very marginally touch on activities that might roundly be recognized as educational? If this is the case (and it seems to be precisely so in more than a few instances), then we would have to say that an athletic program's graduation rate is a mostly useless metric for measuring real educational progress.

So, why do they continue to harp on such measurements?

Because they know most people—thanks in large part to the grave deficiencies of our educational system—have never been forced to ponder the problem of perception and how powerful forces are constantly creating and organizing mental structures designed to mediate between us and the vastness of reality, mediations designed to direct our attentions toward perceptions and interpretations that are invariably amenable to the interests of those very same powerful entities.

Indeed, one of the more common of these elite-imposed suggestions is precisely the idea that there *is no one or any identifiable group of people* imposing frames of interpretation upon the common people; that is, that we are always and everywhere addressing ourselves to the world with a virgin gaze.

Like large revenue-producing college athletic programs, Big Pharma is deeply aware of how little thought most citizens, and even more sadly, most medical professionals give to how "facts" and notions of "reality" enter into their field of consciousness. And they play mercilessly upon this widespread epistemological illiteracy.

Take the PCR test.

Since the dawn of Western medicine, medical diagnostics has been driven by symptomatology; that is, by having a physician cast his experienced eyes upon the physical manifestations of sickness in the patient. No symptoms, no diagnosis. No diagnosis, no treatment.

But what if you are the owner of a business that sells treatments and wants to expand its market share? Or a government leader, who might want to sow panic and division in a population so as to better control them?

Might it not be in each of their interests to generate a proxy of illness, one that would greatly inflate the numbers of those considered "sick" or "dangerous" and sell it to the population as being as grave and important as the real thing?

This is exactly what was done with the PCR tests.

We see a very similar approach in the measurement of vaccine effectiveness. The only truly useful measurements of vaccine effectiveness are whether a) they stop transmission and thus bring an epidemic to an end b) lead to a decrease of overall sickness and mortality.

But what if a company had invested billions of dollars in the development of a vaccine that could do neither of these things?

Well, you simply develop proxy measurements, such as the rise in antibody levels in injected trial subjects—results that may or may not have a proven causal relation with the above-mentioned real measurements of effectiveness—and present them as being flawless indicators of success in disease minimization and eradication. This was, it appears, what was done in the FDA's recent scandalous decision to approve the mRNA vaccines for administration to newborns and toddlers.

We have been told *ad nauseam* that lowering cholesterol is *per se* a good thing. But what if, as Malcolm Kendrick, Naseem Malhotra and others have argued, the line of causality between elevated cholesterol and serious cardiac illness and cardiac illness—arguably one of the most complex and multifactorial maladies a human being can suffer—is not nearly as clear as we have been led to believe?

Then we'd have another case of a proxy indicator—whose promotion not coincidentally enriches pharmaceutical companies greatly—being presented to us as a simple key to resolving an often inscrutably complex problem. And all this doesn't take into account the often considerable side effects that have been shown to accompany the use of statins.

And what about blood pressure and blood pressure medications? Let's assume you are someone who carefully and frequently monitors their blood pressure at home to insure that it remains within normal limits, but finds that when you go to the doctor—where anxiety is always present for many patients and where the prescribed procedures about how to take blood pressure are routinely violated by the hurried office employees—your reading is considerably higher?

Despite the fact that "white coat syndrome" has been well acknowledged in the scientific literature, the patient is often put in the position of having to defend their voluminous record of normal readings at home against the one-time, or every six month, reading taken in the artificial setting of the doctor's office, with all that this implies in terms having to stand up to a doctor who is usually all too ready to use this obvious proxy indicator as a reason to commit the patient to a lifetime of anti-hypertensive medication.

Once you start examining things in this way, the examples are nearly endless.

The elites' ability to flood our consciousness with fragmentary and undigested information has increased exponentially. And they are well aware of, and quite satisfied by, the sense of disorientation this information overload causes in the majority of citizens. Why? Because they know that a disoriented or overwhelmed person is much more likely to grasp at simplistic solutions when they are directed this way.

If we are to regain our rightful protagonism as citizens of a republic we must closely study the mechanics of these processes, starting, in the particular case of public health policy, by addressing the serial abuse of flimsy proxy "evidence" in matters of grave personal and public importance.

1 August 2022

DID HEALTH OFFICIALS ENABLE BIG PHARMA TO DEFRAUD THE GOVERNMENT?

Perhaps no phrase has been used with greater persistence by government officials and government agencies during the last 20 months than "safe and effective."

During this time Drs. Fauci and Walensky have used it again and again in public appearances to summarize the supposedly essential characteristics of the mRNA vaccines that were offered to the American public beginning in January 2021, and forced on them though government and employer mandates starting in the early fall of that same year.

This same description of the mRNA injections has been repeated endlessly in the mainstream media and in public service announcements funded with taxpayer money.

But what if the vaccines were not safe and effective? And what if the government spokespeople and agencies who repeatedly characterized them as such had very good reason to know that these assertions were not actually rooted in empirically demonstrated results?

Would it not be fraudulent to state blithely and repeatedly from government platforms that this was flatly true—thus fattening Pharma revenues—when, in fact, the manufacturers of the product being offered and then imposed upon the American public stated repeatedly that there was no factual basis for making this assertion?

From what I have been able to understand as a non-lawyer, the US legal code sees fraud as something overwhelmingly done *to* the government rather than something committed *by* it.

However, *18 U.S. Code § 201 – Bribery of public officials and witnesses*, would seem to provide at least one possible route for going after government officials who repeatedly made untrue claims about the known safety and effectiveness of the injections.

It states that: "Whoever, being a public official or person selected to be a public official, directly or indirectly, corruptly demands, seeks, receives, accepts, or agrees to receive or accept anything of value personally or for any other person or entity, in return for: **(A)** being influenced in the performance of any official act; **(B) being influenced to commit or aid in committing, or to collude in, or allow, any fraud, or make opportunity for the commission of any fraud, on the United States.**

The Language from Foreign Contracts

As has been noted, US officials repeatedly recurred to the "safe and effective" mantra when seeking to stimulate vaccine uptake among the citizens of this country.

However, in the vaccine contracts Pfizer signed with the European Commission and numerous countries (Albania, Brazil, Colombia, Chile, the Dominican Republic and Peru)—documents which were supposed to have stayed secret but were eventually leaked to the press—the pharmaceutical giant invariably includes the following clause.

"The Participating Member State acknowledges that the Vaccine and materials related to the Vaccine, and their components and constituent materials are being rapidly developed due to the emergency circumstances of the Covid-19 pandemic and will continue to be studied after provision of the Vaccine to the Participating Member States under the APA. **The Participating Member State further acknowledges that the long-term effects and efficacy of the Vaccine are not currently known and that there may be adverse effects of the Vaccine that are not currently known.**"

How can this be squared with the no-room-for-doubt rhetoric of "safe and effective" which we have heard *ad nauseam* over the last 20 months?

It obviously can't.

It will be suggested, not without reason, that these foreign contracts may or may not be representative of the contract that Pfizer signed with the US government and that we cannot therefore assume similar statements are found in the yet to be leaked contract or contracts signed with the US government.

But given the size and importance of the US market and the enormous negative consequences for Pfizer in the case of clear-cut problems with either safety or efficacy (which have in fact occurred) there is every reason to assume the US contract(s) contain this same out-clause regarding the unproven nature of the injections' safety and efficacy.

One would have to believe, moreover, that Drs. Fauci and Walensky would have been privy to the language on the lack of clear proof about safety and efficacy included in the US contract. And yet they repeatedly told the public, directly, and in the case of Walensky, indirectly through materials released to the public by her agency, that the injections were, without a doubt, safe and effective.

Which brings us to the matter of their "**being influenced to commit or aid in committing, or to collude in, or allow, any fraud, or make opportunity for the commission of any fraud, on the United States.**"

Presuming the wording on the lack of substantial proof for the safety and efficacy of the injections was present in the US Pfizer contract, and they were aware of it, their repeated assertions to the contrary in public and through the organs they controlled are mendacious in the extreme.

And it would seem self-evident that—and this perhaps gets us closer to the matter of colluding in fraud—their "safe and effective" rhetoric greased the skids for the widespread acceptance in political and media circles of the massive new vaccine contract Pfizer signed with the US government this past June.

The larger question is whether they or anyone else in the leadership cadres of the NAID, the CDC of the FDA can be said to have "directly or indirectly" **demanded, sought, received, accepted or agreed to receive or accept anything of value personally** in exchange for their serial misrepresentation of the known safety and performance profile of the Pfizer jabs.

It would seem at the very least that we are looking at a clear case of highly organized lying. Whether this lying rises to the level of colluding with a corporate entity to commit fraud against the US government remains unclear.

In light of this, now would seem to be a time, if nothing else, to redouble our efforts to obtain as much of the correspondence between Pfizer and top US health officials as we can, and to ask people much more legally expert than me if there is any basis for pursuing this putative case of fraud in the courts.

9 August 2022

MY GRATITUDE FOR THE APOLOGIES AND
SINCERE EXPRESSIONS OF REGRET

Dear Friends and Valued Acquaintances:

Sorry it's taken me so long to write. Frankly I've been over-whelmed by all the signs of love and sincere regret so many of you have recently sent my way.

While I've never been a huge fan of group messages, I believe in this case it is (someone once told me it is never wise to postpone the expression of gratitude) probably the most expeditious way of thanking you for the outpouring of support and compassion you've directed to me and other Covid heretics now that the mainstream discourse on this "unprecedented threat to our safety"™ lies in tatters on the ground before us.

So here goes.

I'd like to send a special note of thanks to all those friends and family members who, after sniggering behind my back that I had gone off my rocker, or had suddenly become an unthinking and selfish Trumpite, sent their sincere apologies for what they said about me, and how I had fallen into mindlessly and obsessively repeating Q-Anon memes.

I am especially grateful for the words of regret I've received from those among this same group that brought the logic of medieval witch-shunning and apartheid to family gatherings and friendships. It's so nice to see that you now realize the fire you were playing with and have all made solemn and quite public pledges to apologize to those you ostracized on the basis of insti-tutionalized superstitions and to never go down that sad and divisive road again.

Most of all, I'd like to thank you for the way you have all graciously admitted that the truth of what I told you repeatedly from the beginning based on my reading of the FDA's own briefing reports on the vaccines (that there was never any scientific evidence that the injections would stop infection or transmission) as well as what has been clear since the leaking in 2021 of the numerous contracts between Pfizer and sovereign governments: there was no available science to back the repeated Government claims that the vaccines were "safe and effective."

I'd like to send a special shout-out to my doctor friends who apparently never took the time to read any of the multiple scientific studies on the efficacy of masks and proven vaccine capabilities that I sent them over the past 30 months and who preferred to respond, on the few times when they did at all, with mocking one-liners and admonitions like "Stay in your lane Tom."

The way each and every one of them has now personally acknowledged the truth of these things as well as the fact that the PCR tests were wildly unreliable, that the idea of massive asymptomatic transmission was a chimera, that social distancing was useless, and that the vaccines have done nothing to stop infection and may, in fact, be promoting it, has been heartwarming.

For these sincere expressions of rectification and regret I will be forever grateful. Moreover, they give me great faith going forward that the medical profession, having recognized its ingrained tendency to substitute Pharma-supplied slogans for the careful review of ever-evolving empirical realities, is poised for a true humanistic renaissance in the realm of patient care.

To my "progressive" former editors in both the US and Spain who decided that my counter-current reflections on Covid starting in March of 2020—almost all of which have now been proven true—were toxic enough to earn me marginalization or excommunication from their list of contributors, I am thankful for the way you have acknowledged how you were taken in by the fear porn aimed your way and have undertaken rigorous investigations aimed at explaining to your readers what happened, and insuring that you will never engage in hysteria-induced sloganeering and personnel purges like this again.

To my former colleagues at the university who hooted me down on the internal faculty listserv with the intoxicated brio of stone-throwing Jacobins when I simply posted the CDC's and the WHO's own words and approved studies on the effectiveness and use of masks in public settings, or when I merely shared the actual death rate per age tranche (as determined by the CDC) of those infected by the virus in the Spring and Summer of 2020, I want to thank you for the many kind and sincere words of regret and repair you have conveyed to me.

My cup runneth over when I think of all the remorseful words and bridge-building sentiments that I have received from the administration of the same university which once arrogantly dismissed my efforts to inform them about the actual known capabilities of masks and PCR tests early on, and spent much of the last two years imprisoning students who had little or no risk from the virus while encouraging the development of a snitch culture among them and, of course, mandating that they get a vaccine that would do next to nothing for them or the community, but would definitely raise their chances of having a serious adverse event.

All this while they fattened the institution's bottom line by charging full tuition at a time when all the very expensive extracurricular activities that are so much a part of today's university experience were felicitously disappeared from the debit side of their ledgers.

And who could forget the way they presented members of the staff and faculty with an ultimatum to take the experimental and useless shots or get fired, even when these employees could present abundant evidence of antibodies from previous infection, and/or a letter from a licensed physician saying that the demand to vaccinate in his or her particular case failed the most basic tests of medical necessity or individual safety.

I can only be grateful that they are, along with other heavily-endowed institutions, taking time out from the urgent task of suppressing free speech to spearhead a national movement to indemnify the students they grifted, as well as the millions of people, like those at their institutions who lost their jobs for having the ability to see through the blizzard of Pharma-led and government amplified propaganda and stand for the essential idea of bodily sovereignty. The billions you will pay out of the gains you made while maintaining high tuitions and greatly limiting student services will be much appreciated.

My heart sings when I hear all of the ways that leaders at school districts across the country are expressing remorse for what they did to children under the guise of protecting them from a virus that could do them little or no harm, and for which they were known, from the mid-spring of 2020 onward, to not serve as important vectors of transmission.

And then—and here again my soul takes flight—there are the profuse and never-ending *mea culpas* from the teachers unions, like the one in New York City, that not only insured that students would wither cognitively and emotionally before their screens at home (that is, if one was readily available in the house where they live), but also colluded with the city's Department of Education to deny—in apparent violation of federal law—religious exemptions to some 99 percent of the people who requested them.

That they are now taking responsibility for what they have done to the defenseless children, and are welcoming the ostracized teachers back to work with both affection and considerable financial recompense for lost wages is truly heartwarming.

I am sure that there are many, many other people who were wrong about almost everything on Covid who, in the spirit of maintaining a sense of moral rigor or exercising basic adult responsibility-taking, are staying up late to compose messages of contrition, and thinking of how best to offer financial restitution to the people whose lives they harmed.

These are harms they committed out of a desire to either not think too deeply, or to simply avoid being seen as being complicit with those that the media and all the cool people around them were identifying as ethical and intellectual deviants.

As their further messages of love and healing flow toward me and my fellow demonized citizens, I will do my best to acknowledge and celebrate them in the way I've done above.

With gratitude:
Tom

16 August 2022

HOW WE LOST AGENCY AND ACQUIESCED TO POWER

Twenty-five years ago, I moved with my wife and three children to the type of prosperous inner-ring suburb—with its tree-lined streets and excellent public schools—that I thought I'd never be able to afford on my professor's salary. But thanks to a dip in the market and a timely loan from my parents, we were able to buy a small house not far from the center of town. I was exultant. And for the first 4-5 years or so of our time there, little if anything broke my personal spell of happiness and gratitude.

In the years immediately following September 11th, however, I began to notice social attitudes in friends and certain public figures that troubled me, attitudes that I now view as having lain the groundwork for the generally meek acceptance of the tyrannies that have been recently been visited upon us, as well as the tendency to quickly sign off on the many attempts being made today to undermine the legitimacy of some of our more important social conventions and institutions.

As I look back, two particular incidents come to mind.

Upon moving to town we joined a church, as much as anything else, to ensure that our children acquire some familiarity with the religious culture that had, in greater or lesser measure, done so much to shape the moral and cosmological outlook of the family members that had preceded them into this world.

In the absence of a common family lexicon, we thought, intergenerational communication often withers, leaving children bereft of vertical referents and thus much more at the mercy of whatever ideas often predatorially-inclined peers and corporations cast in their direction. This was something we wanted to head off, and we believed that giving our kids the opportunity to, if nothing else, locate themselves both ethno-culturally, and in the broader continuum of Western history, might be of considerable worth.

We joined the most liberal Catholic church in the area, one with an active gay ministry and very strong programs for the homeless as well as a mission program in Haiti.

All went well, until the US invaded Iraq, and in the prayers for the faithful we were asked week after week, to "pray for the American troops who were bringing peace to the Middle East." There was nary a word or a thought, however, for the tens of thousands of Iraqis that had been injured or killed by our unprovoked invasion.

One day after mass I finally confronted the pastor and asked why, in light of the fact that the Pope had said quite clearly that the US attack on Iraq could in no way be considered a just war, he continued to celebrate the acts of US soldiers and simply ignore the unthinkable tragedies they had wrought in the lives of millions of Iraqis. After stumbling around for words, he finally said, "I agree with you. But, lots of people in our parish have relatives in the service and I really don't want to offend them."

At about the same time, a very big parcel of land became available adjacent to the historic center of the town. The town government began a much-announced public process of deciding on the best way to utilize it.

It soon became clear, however, that citizen hearings were a complete sham, a reality made apparent by: a) the fact that the town was already promoting a developer's fully hatched plan on its own websites and b) the sight of the town's economic development director engaging in smiley chit-chat with the principle of the development company on the auditorium balcony, high above the common folk seeking to have their concerns addressed.

During the weeks of the hearing process, I would talk to friends and to the parents of the other kids on my children's sports team about what I saw as the rank corruption of the process. Most of the time, I just got blank stares.

But those who did respond invariably said something like "So, I don't get it, are you for it or against it?"

What virtually no one seemed to comprehend, despite my using all manner of restatements and circumlocutions to express it, was that I was not talking about the inherent desirability, or not, of the project, *but rather the quality of the process* being used to decide on an issue that would shape our community physically and fiscally for many years to come.

I was flabbergasted. Outside of the small minority of us who were actively demanding more transparency, no one in our "nice" community had the least interest in the processes established to safeguard our inherent rights as citizens and taxpayers. All that mattered, it seemed, was that we might now have another cool place to shop and dine in the middle of town.

"Was it always this way?" I asked myself.

Did ostensibly progressive pastors, in possession of papal teachings that gave them enormous leeway for challenging their congregations on the essential matter of the mass killing of human beings, always defer to the perceived sensitivities of those in their flock?

Was the duty to safeguard citizen power and civic structures and pass them on intact to our children always seen as a stylized and archaic adjunct to the pursuit of more and better customer options?

After much thought, I decided that "No," this was not always the case. Something essential had changed. But what was it?

In my view the thing that changed was our nearly wholesale exchange of the ethos of citizenship, with its concern for the preservation of abstract principles, for that of the consumer.

Whereas, the citizen is charged quite explicitly with stopping and reflecting on the present in light of what has been said, done and established in the past, the consumer lives in a present conditioned by the imperative to take a headlong lunge into what he has been told is an ever-expanding and ever-improving future. As Zygmunt Bauman said in his essential *Tourists and Vagabonds:*

"For the consumers in the society of consumers, being on the move—searching, looking for, not-finding-it or more exactly not-finding-it-yet is not a malaise, but the promise of bliss; perhaps it is the bliss itself. Theirs is the kind of traveling hopefully which makes arriving into a curse.... Not so much the greed to acquire and possess, nor the gathering of wealth in its material tangible sense, as the excitement of a new and unprecedented sensation is the name of the consumer game. Consumers are first and foremost gatherers of *sensations*; they are collectors of *things* only in a secondary and derivative sense."

Though consumer culture often presents itself as wildly progressive, and frequently presents citizen culture as stodgy and undynamic, in many ways just the opposite is true.

Viewed in the most basic sense, citizenship is a vocation rooted in the acceptance of controlled conflict, and the implied belief that that same refereed clash of articulated interests will, slowly but surely, lead us all to greater social advancement.

In contrast, consumer culture largely obviates the question of power through its presentation of the world as a vast emporium to which any and all can accede with a minimum of difficulty. The key, as we are constantly told in large and small ways, is to not throw sand in the gears of the marvelous machine of inexorable progress and to instead work within its self-evidently sage and moral rules to acquire your personal seat at the table of plenty.

That the ever titillating and ever phagocytic "spectacle" of consumerism as Debord called it might be heedlessly disappearing important debates about what it means to be conscious, moral and human, as well as about how the disappearance of these essential conversations probably favors the interests of those already in possession of undue parcels of social and economic power, is never brought up.

Neither is the stark and paradoxical fact that no great leap forward in social welfare has ever been generated by a program of mass conformity to purely transactional dictates. Quite the opposite, in fact.

A deeply pernicious byproduct of this enveloping "don't rock the boat" ethos is what the poet and philosopher Robert Bly called the "Sibling Society," a place where adults actively eschew the responsibilities invested in them by dint of their age, skill, or fortuitous social ascent.

To consciously exercise social responsibility is to necessarily court and provoke conflict and disappointment in those around you. And while it is never wise to reflexively ignore the negative reactions one harvests from taking well-meditated stands within the family or in the public square, it is less wise still to proactively retreat from the field of conflict simply to keep the peace.

But keeping the peace at all costs has, it seems, become a sacred and unquestionable goal among large parts of our society, especially among its more credentialed sectors. This pose engenders a widespread spirit of acquiescence to power, and an indifference to its often very damaging actions.

It is this same cultural outlook that has generated a sizable cohort of parents who believe their first task as parents is to please their children, something that consequently leaves no small number of their offspring without aspirational models and useful guidance as they make their way toward adulthood.

It is also an attitude that has greatly enabled the ceaseless bullying of cancel culture at our centers of teaching and learning.

And finally it is this disposition, this failure to assume and make use of social and moral capital that one presumably accrues in the course of life that, in my view, made the elites' task of imposing its various and wholly undemocratic articles of tyranny upon us during the past 30 months rather easy.

Big power loves nothing more than a population that is largely indifferent to its own social and political agency, where adults have divested themselves of the vertical influence bequeathed to them for the purpose of molding the young, and if circumstances require it, imposing their will upon them. When adults abandon this essential task they send out two screaming messages.

The first, which quickly arrives at the eyes and ears of their children, is that there is really no higher life law than the pursuit of material comfort through acquiescence to the *status quo*, an order whose "laws" have, of course, been inordinately shaped by the ultra-powerful.

The second, which quickly arrives to the eyes and ears of the same ultra-powerful is that if many of the most privileged members of what we might call the aspirant class below them are unwilling to assume the mantle of adulthood in their homes and communities, then they've got very little to worry about when they next find it opportune to strip us of a few more of the prerogatives that, according to our Constitution, belong to us in perpetuity.

Is this really the record we wish to leave in regard to our defense of the cultural gifts bequeathed to us by our elders?

21 August 2022

THE PERSISTENCE OF COVID
CRUELTY ON CAMPUS

When I entered the field of nationalism studies 35 years ago, it was characterized by a clear tilt toward two important ideological postures.

The first, a product of the rise of Marxist historiography in Western universities in the first three to four decades following the Second World War, was the belief that insurgent nationalist movements are, much more often than not, set in motion by mobilizations of the common people.

The second, a product of the early 20th century invention of the discipline of political science—a project essentially designed to provide a rational-sounding and elite-friendly apologetics for the brute exercise of domestic and imperial power—was that the best way to understand the rise of such movements was to focus primarily on, what else, the lives and actions of those who had spent their lives immersed in the world of elections, political parties and other official means of marshaling social power.

As luck would have it, however, this paradigm was in the process of being turned on its head as I got into the game, thanks in large part to the publication in 1983 of a remarkable book by the Cornell historian and specialist in east Asian cultures, Benedict Anderson. In his *Imagined Communities*, Anderson traces the development of the modern idea of the nation from its inception in the early 16th century up until the latter half of the 1900s.

Reading it, two things become crystal clear. The first is that the idea of creating new national collectives *always* manifests itself first in the minds of an often quite small lettered elite that imagines what the new entity will be like and that, in the hope of rendering it real, sets out to create and distribute its guiding myths.

The second, which flows axiomatically from the first, is that politics, understood in the way we now typically conceive of it, is almost always a distant *trailing edge* of these robust and quite consciously undertaken programs of cultural production.

In the early 1990s the brilliant Israel scholar Itamar Even-Zohar seconded Anderson's emphasis on the role of elites and what he calls their acts of "culture-planning" in the creation and maintenance of nations, and indeed, all other insurgent movements of social identity.

Using his mastery of 15 languages and the access it gave him to the archives of many distinct national and social movements through time he sought to identify the tropes, cultural models and institutional practices that are common to the construction of virtually all such social projects, techniques whose central aim is always that of generating what he calls a state of "proneness" among the general population.

"Culture provides cohesion to both a factual or a potential collective entity. This is achieved by creating a disposition of allegiance among those who adhere to the repertoire of cultural goods. At the same time, this acquired cohesion generates a validated disposition of distinction, i.e., a state of separateness from other entities. What is generally meant by `cohesion' is a state where a widely spread sense of solidarity, or togetherness, exists among a group of people, which consequently does not require acts enforced by sheer physical power. The basic, key concept to such cohesion is readiness, or proneness. Readiness (proneness) is a mental disposition which propels people to act in many ways which otherwise may be contrary to their 'natural inclinations.' For example, going to war ready to be killed in fighting against some other group would be the ultimate case, amply repeated throughout human history".

To accept Even-Zohar's rich transhistorical and transnational rendering of the way collective entities have been initiated, grown and maintained over the centuries is to begin looking at culture, and with it politics, in an entirely new way.

It does away with the admittedly appealing idea that any new concept of social reality ever emerges organically from the masses. Moreover, it presumes as completely natural and unexceptional the idea of collusion between elites in the realm of creating acceptable ideals of social behavior.

And in this way, it shows the common contemporary accusation that one is a "conspiracy theorist" for what it is: a desperate attempt on the part of those same elites, or their paid agents, to stop pointed inquiries into the way power works when the rest of us aren't looking.

Indeed, Even-Zohar's work suggests that few things occupy as much space in the minds of powerful elites than inventing ways to make us believe that what is good for their interests is also good for our own.

If you've followed me this far you might be asking yourself, "What does all this have to do with the topic announced in the title of this article?"

I would say, "Quite a lot."

The Continuation of Covid Draconianism Campus

Over the last several months the senseless and damaging Covid restrictions have steadily been repealed all over this country and all over the world. There is one important realm, however, where this has not broadly been the case: our colleges and universities, especially those seen as occupying the highest rungs of our educational hierarchy.

From the point of view of disease control, the persistence of these outdated and manifestly ineffective Covid rules at colleges obviously makes no sense. In fact, it never did. College students were always among the people least likely to be affected in a negative way by the virus.

But what if disease prevention is not what it is really all about?

What if the goal is, instead, to culture-plan for a concept of the human ontology that naturalizes, not the individually-oriented sense of dignity, volition and resilience that has animated the search for meaning in the West since the dawn of modernity in the 16th century, but instead one that speaks to the logic of the feudalism that preceded it?

A feudal system presumes that the only way one can move ahead safely in the world is to establish a relationship of dependence with a powerful other who, in exchange for his protection, is granted unfettered access to the bodies (for sex, for soldiering and for labor) of his vassals and their families.

If a cultural transformation of this magnitude is indeed the goal of our present mega-elites—and there are very good reasons to believe it just might be the case—then the continuation of nonsensical Covid rules on campus makes perfect sense.

Never in history has the pipeline connecting the well-credentialed to the prime centers of social power been more consolidated and impermeable than now.

The results are there for all to see in our so-called quality media, and especially (but in no ways exclusively) in the present US presidential administration. The examples of young, well-credentialed, if thinly educated and—paradox of paradoxes considering their rhetorical fixations with diversity and cosmopolitanism—deeply provincial young people in high places can be seen all around us.

And yet these callow provincials in government, and in the media that so often presents the inbred banality of their thought-processes as wisdom, are convinced they are changing the world. And in some ways, they are right.

While their policies in both the domestic and international realms lack anything that could be roundly be described as constructively unifying in intent or effect, they are very good at one thing: sniffing after power, seizing it, and distributing the fruits among those whom they see as sharing their same sense of credentialed righteousness.

At the same time, however, they seem to be aware on another level—a case of the impostor syndrome?—of the self-evidently dead-end and divisive nature of their woke social postulates, and the ridiculousness of their attempts to present themselves—as the impenitent imperialists and war-mongers they are—as morally enlightened protectors of the great family of man.

And this is where the continuation of senseless Covid policies on campus comes in.

A minimally reflexive person might ask him or herself if there might be something inherently flawed in the policies, such as they are, that they are foisting on the American people and the world, whether something other than the supposed uncomprehending idiocy of the unwashed might be driving the hostility regularly hurled in their direction.

But for a group raised on trophies for all, grade inflation and a continuous diet of "You can get it if you really want it" sermons, none of this applies. Rather, it is a simple question of numbers. Right now, as they see it, there are simply more benighted dummies out there than good people like themselves.

The answer?

Redouble efforts to ensure that the maximum number of credentialed eligibles in society ally with their faction.

How?

By making sure that all of them receive what Heinrich Böll memorably called the "Host of the Beast"—a sort of solidarity-fostering Eucharist of evil—in *Billiards at Half-Past Nine*, his masterful interrogation of the culture of Nazism.

Human beings hate to be proven wrong. And credentialed humans even more so than the rest. Consequently, they will go to mind-bending extremes to sustain that their clearly equivocal actions were, in fact, heartily justified. Moreover, misery truly does love company.

When faced with the choice of admitting to past errors and gullibility, or seeking to induce others to share in their misfortune—thus relativizing their shame at having been duped—surprisingly many people will choose the latter.

By force-vaccinating today's college students, our credentialed would-be revolutionaries are placing those same students in the position of having to take a difficult stand in the face of overwhelming social pressure, something that, owing to the fact that many of their parents deprived them of the ability to develop independent moral reasoning through the game of trial and error, most of them are woefully unprepared to do.

If at a later date they do develop a sense of moral autonomy that leads them to question how and why they gave their bodily sovereignty for no discernibly valid reason, the mix of anger and shame inside them is sure to be considerable.

But given their credentialed status, and the social advantages it will by then have probably conferred to them, how many will be willing or able to face those troubling emotions with equanimity and courage?

My guess is fairly few.

Far more likely is that these people, like those tortured in fraternity and sports team hazing rituals, will seek to refashion their capitulation to the culture of ambient cruelty into a badge of honor and a sign of their worthiness to be included among the elect.

No good reason for leaving cruel Covid absurdities in place at our colleges and universities?

Think again.

When considered in terms of the goal of ensuring a future flow of cadres for a culture-planning project designed, it seems, to convince the many of the "naturalness" of their helplessness before the designs of the few, it makes perfect sense.

23 August 2022

TESTIMONY, TRUTH AND POWER

The search for truth is always difficult and deeply enmeshed with questions of social power. As the old saying about history being written by the victors suggests, the powerful really do have an inordinately strong ability to propagate and control what passes for reality in the public square. And, as I've suggested before, they use this prerogative to assiduously produce images and stories that portray them and the policies they advance in the most positive possible light.

Just as important as their capacity to propagate schemas of "reality" is their ability to disappear those discourses that threaten to undermine their effective control of what is real such as, say, the murder of innocent peasants that enables a given subset of the overprivileged class to further expand their realm of pecuniary and political control within a culture.

This disappearance service is most often provided by professional historians and journalists who, while they enjoy slathering themselves with encomiums like "intellectually impartial" and "fiercely independent," are, more often than not, quite content to not show the public what the powerful do not want that public to see.

It was in response to the systematic erasures of past crimes and atrocities that the genre of testimonial literature arose in Latin America during the last 3 or so decades of the 20th century. The idea was to eliminate to the highest degree possible the role of clearly corrupted mediating institutions in the creation of guiding social stories, or discourses.

How?

By seeking out those who had survived the violence visited on them by the wealthy and their willing accomplices in the state, listening to their stories, and making those stories available to audiences outside the immediate sociological space of the victims. In this way, it was held, the powerless would preserve history that might otherwise be forgotten, engage the dignifying process of talking back to their tormentors, and remind those in power in other places of the need to remedy their plight.

What's not to like?

Isn't this, in many ways, what those of us who write about the hidden ravages of the Covid response are effectively trying to do during these times of rampant social destruction and institutional rot?

It would seem so.

Unfortunately, however, not all movements remain true to the original visions of their founders. As the laudable ethos of testimonial literature spread from departments of Hispanic Studies to other humanities disciplines in US universities, something got lost in the process.

What began as an attempt to broaden our understanding of the past became something very different in the hands of the increasingly woke offspring of the original proponents of testimonialism. This something was characterized by two troubling, and if we think about it, patently ridiculous presumptions.

The first is that those who have been victims of corrupt mediating institutions always speak the unqualified truth. The second is that these witnesses to past crimes and those that promote their voices are themselves congenitally free of the base desires for power and influence that have animated the lives of those they see as their tormentors.

Ask yourself. Does having been a victim insure that one will not ever use every tool at one's disposal, including testimonialism itself, to fatten one's account of social power and prestige?

Of course not.

Yet as we look around, this corrosive notion—which is gleefully heedless of the abundant evidence of the human tendency toward self-dealing and self-deception—goes largely unchallenged in our public conversations. And in the few instances when it is pointed out that a self-anointed victim just might also be an untruthful and shameless seeker of power, those raising the question are trampled by organized online mobs.

As a result, people of intellectual good faith, which is to say, those dedicated to calibrating the good and the bad in all intellectual and social proposals regardless of their tribal provenance, are increasingly afraid to raise their heads above the parapet.

More importantly and perniciously, it has consolidated—to use a term developed in the context of Spain's numerous 19th century military coups—a culture of the *pronunciamiento* within the civic, intellectual and scientific spheres of our society.

If "I" "pronounce" that those who don't pursue justice for my self-designated sexual, medical or identitary cause with the fervor that "I" and my chosen allies have decided it merits, then "they" can quite rightly be labeled a malicious hater and danger to the social peace. And if they refuse to accept that appellation lying down, "I" and my cadres have every "right" to call in the mob and effectively banish them from the public square.

It gets worse.

The unfortunate lessons of this bastardized deployment of testimonialism have not been lost on the powerful who are, of course, always looking for new methods for expanding their purchase of social and financial capital.

Seeing the rampant power-garnering success of online *pronunciamientos* during the last 6 years or so, they have adopted it as one of their prime tools of governance. Why go to the bother of making arguments when you can simply trot out your own sovereign and unassailable personal "testimony" of the truth?

We are thus treated to the ongoing reality of a feedback loop between these ultra-powerful movers and shakers and the thirty percent army of authoritarian "liberal" brownshirts who are inordinately well-represented in our culture-making institutions.

When you challenge a position proffered by one side or another of this two-headed monster on its merits, they feel no need to respond to the query in any meaningful way. Rather, they simply remit the questioner to the supposedly unassailable authority of the other head of the beast. The goal of this repetitive insider game of tag is, of course, to convince those of us on the outside of the futility of challenging their edicts. And unfortunately, it works with many.

But what happens to those who, after all these attempts to cow them into irrelevance, continue to ask impertinent questions?

Well, here is where we see perhaps the most grotesque appropriation of testimonialism's nobly-inspired practices: the spectacle of the most powerful among us portraying themselves as the world's ultimate victims, laying the groundwork in this way, for the effective banishment of those who refuse to bow down before their evidence-free, or evidence-challenged personal renditions of the "truth."

This is what Fauci did when he declared himself the poor, unfairly embattled emissary of "science itself." And this has been what the Biden cabal, fully backed, no less, by the enormous repressive apparatus of the Deep State, has done at every turn, first with January 6th protestors, then with the unvaccinated and now with the seeming majority of citizens who refuse to recognize the providential nature of his presidency.

Make no mistake about it. These are dog whistles designed to prime the 30 percent army of cancellers to work their magic in the upcoming campaign to further take down the non-compliant.

Testimonio, or testimonialism as I have rendered it in English, was a very noble and necessary attempt to salvage and distribute the disappeared history of the many victims of military government and economic power in Latin America's recent history. After it rightly gained a foothold in the American academy, its laudable emphasis on widening the chorus of voices involved in the making of the historical record caused it to spread like wildfire to other humanistic disciplines. Its fruits were many.

But somewhere along the way, this drive to broaden our understanding of the past was commandeered by academic cynics who saw in its exaltation of the personal a way to effectively marshal power without going through the arduous work of having to convince others of the wisdom of either their interpretations or their policy prescriptions.

More alarmingly, these same cynics began openly encouraging students to eschew argument and rely on the allegedly unassailable reality of their personal stories, as well as their personal, if often grotesquely ill-informed, interpretations of the past.

"Like, I feel..." is now arguably the single most uttered phrase in our college classrooms today, and it would seem, in an ever-growing percentage of our "educated" young.

Since these students have often not been forced to structure arguments in the crucible of the classroom (being allowed instead to substitute their personal testimonies rooted in the flotsam and jetsam of popular culture and woke orthodoxies for ordered argumentative discourse), they do not know how or why they should demand such well-honed explanations from others.

"If, like, Fauci, like, says it's safe and effective and the President, like, says we need to do it to protect the vulnerable, like, what more do you want?. Are you, like, one of those anti-vaxxers or something?"

This virtual dialogue between no-reason issuers of edicts and young citizens who don't demand arguments forms an unvirtuous circle...to the benefit, of course, of those already in possession of power.

We must begin to more stubbornly stick to our guns when both the powerful old, and the insouciant young, spring the "Agree-with-my-sound-bite-version-of-the-truth-or-be-banished" gambit on us. Yes, they will amp up the volume to try and get us to cower and fold. We need to be stubborn and conflictive with them in ways that many of us never wanted, or believed we could be.

If we do otherwise, we are, I honestly think, looking at the end of both democratic republicanism and the ideal of pursuing truth through study.

7 September 2022

THE LEFT FAILED THE COVID TEST BADLY

L
ike every other important social phenomenon, propaganda regimes have historical genealogies. For example, a very strong case could be made that the ongoing, and sad to admit, largely successful Covid propaganda onslaught under which we now live can trace its roots back, as I suggested in an earlier essay, to the two so-called demonstration wars (the Panama Invasion and the First Gulf War waged by George Bush Sr.

To recapitulate, the American elites were badly stung by the country's defeat in Vietnam. In it, they rightly saw a considerable curtailment of what they had come to see as their divine right since the end of WWII: the ability to intervene as they saw fit in any country not explicitly covered by the Soviet nuclear umbrella.

And in their analysis of that failure, they correctly alighted to the role that the media—by simply bringing the tawdry and ignoble reality of the war into our living rooms—had played in undermining citizen willingness to engage in such fruitless, costly and savage adventures in the future.

With his massive military build-up and heavy support of proxies in Latin America in the eighties, Ronald Reagan took the first steps toward recovering this lost elite prerogative.

But it was not until the administration of George Bush Sr. and the two conflicts mentioned above that, as he himself exultantly put it in the wake of his pitiless slaughter of some 100,000 poorly equipped Iraqis, we "kicked the Vietnam Syndrome once and for all."

Bush knew what he was talking about, and it wasn't necessarily, or even primarily, military force or prowess.

What had largely limited Reagan to proxy wars during eight years in office were two things. The first was a citizenry that still had fresh memories of the debacle in Southeast Asia. The second, and arguably more important one was a press corps with on-the-ground familiarity with the reality of these conflicts that continued to challenge him on both their morality and strategic efficacy.

Bush and his team, which as you'll remember included one Richard Cheney at Defense, made remedying this problem of war-hesitancy one of the central aims of his presidency. Experimenting with new media management techniques was not a strategic sideshow of these conflicts, but rather their *prime goal*.

The Panama invasion was followed in quick succession by the Gulf War, where press coverage put heavy emphasis on the opinions of US military figures and their explanations of the technical genius of American-made military technology. In this way, the war was presented to Americans as a sort of exciting video game characterized by flashes of light in the night and precision attacks devoid of any bloodshed and death.

This process of desensitizing of the media, and from there, the American people to the horrendous human effects of war-making culminated in the revolting spectacle, on January 30th, 1991, of reporters chuckling along with General Norman Schwartzkopf as he joked while showing them videos of supposed "smart bombs" killing people like ants from the safety of 30,000 feet.

Having received no coordinated pushback from anyone with power about this degrading treatment of human life and the American people, they tripled down and went full Manichaean after September 11th.

Why not?

With Reagan's repeal of the fairness Doctrine in 1987 and Bill Clinton's Telecommunications Act of 1996 never had the media been a) concentrated in so few hands b) so beholden to the government regulation for the continuance of the super-profitability generated through this consolidation c) debilitated by the internet-induced collapse of the newspaper business model and thus d) less obligated to take into account the concerns and interests of a broad spectrum of the American people.

It was now truly, as George Bush Jr said, a matter of "You're either with us or against us," us of course being the war-making government (including the Deep State) along with its slavishly loyal media mouthpieces. If you believed the maniacal presumptions of the US response to September 11th were flawed, and said so, you could in this new environment, expect to be the object of well-coordinated attacks on your character.

Never once did the administration call for restraint in such attacks, nor did any administration figures remind people of the importance of the supposedly American value of everyone's right to be respectfully heard.

Seeing the exhaustion of the Bush brand after the Iraq debacle, the Deep State switched party allegiances in the run-up to the 2008 election. And it has stayed firmly on the side of the so-called "left" ever since, encouraging the use of Bush-Cheney-style government-media mobbing against those who might dare to question the motives of the sainted warmonger Obama, or, the "logic" of trying to reduce the problems of racism by promoting it through identity politics.

The efficiency of such mob-style takedown tactics was greatly enhanced by the dramatic expansion of social media platforms in the Obama and Trump years.

It is no exaggeration to say that a person born in 1990 or later has little if any understanding of what it means to disagree in detail and in good faith with someone whose political and/or social ideals are different than their own. Nor what it means to feel obligated to respond to the claims of others with careful factual refutations.

What they do know, because it's mostly all that they have seen from their supposed betters, is that to argue is to seek the destruction of one's interlocutor, and failing that, to make sure his or her arguments are impeded from circulating freely in our shared civic spaces. The ever-increasing dialectical poverty of those who have been socialized and educated in this environment is evident to anyone who has served as a classroom instructor during the last quarter century.

A sanctuary for the weary

While most people seemed to want to pretend that nothing new was happening, that the collaboration between media and government had always been this extreme, many of us did not. We had memories. And we knew the field of "thinkable thought" was dramatically smaller in 2005 than in 1978. And we knew it had become much, much smaller in

2018 than it was in 2005. In our search for answers we turned to media critics and scholars of media history. We also turned to the writings of journalist-activists with both interest and insight into these matters.

When it came to this last group, I found myself drawn principally to what might be termed leftist anti-imperialists. Reading them, I widened my understanding of how elites and their chosen "experts" manage information flows, and constantly seek to shrink the parameters of acceptable opinion on foreign policy issues.

Two years ago last March, however, my sense of intellectual kinship with this subset of thinkers suddenly became very strained.

We were facing what I immediately recognized as the largest and most aggressive perception management campaign in recent times, and perhaps in the history of the world. One, moreover, that was utilizing all the techniques employed during the previous two to three decades to insure citizen allegiance to US war-making.

And yet in the face of it, almost all my go-to people on propaganda analysis had little or nothing to say. And when I sent contributions outlining my doubts about the congruence of the emergent Covid discourse to places that had generally welcomed my analyses of pro-war propaganda, suddenly there was hesitation on the other end.

And the passage of time has cured nothing. Indeed, the only things these people said on the subject down the road—that is, if they addressed Covid at all—was to underscore the unprecedented severity of the situation and harp on Trump's supposedly disastrous handling of it.

There was virtually no daylight between the opinions of these people and the feckless liberals they, as true-blue leftists, always claimed to disdain. And on it went, for the entire two years of the Covid panic.

A week or so ago, John Pilger, arguably one of the brightest and more persistent leftist analysts of establishment propaganda, published "Silencing the lambs: How propaganda works" on his website and then at a number of progressive news outlets.

In it, he repeats all sorts of well-known ideas and concepts. There's a reference to Leni Riefenstahl and how she believed the bourgeoisie are those most amenable to influence campaigns, a reminder of Julian Assange's horrendous and undeserved fate, much deserved praise for Harold Pinter's absolutely extraordinary if largely ignored Nobel acceptance speech, and an intelligent discussion about how our media studiously refuses to tell us about anything that went on between Russia and the West, and Russia and Ukraine between 1990 and February of this year.

The underlying thesis of the piece is that while constantly pushing elite-approved messages is a key element of propaganda, so too is the strategic disappearance of essential historical realities and truths.

All good stuff. Indeed, all themes that I have written about with frequency and conviction over the years.

Toward the end piece Pilger asks the following rhetorical question: "When will real journalists stand up?"

And a few lines later, after providing us with a list of where to find the few outlets and journalists that know how to dissect the elite's informational misdirection plays, he adds:

"And when will writers stand up, as they did against the rise of fascism in the 1930s? When will film-makers stand up, as they did against the Cold War in the 1940s? When will satirists stand up, as they did a generation ago?" Having soaked for 82 years in a deep bath of righteousness that is the official version of the last world war, isn't it time those who are meant to keep the record straight declared their independence and decoded the propaganda? The urgency is greater than ever".

Reading this final flourish while remembering the lamb-like silence of John Pilger in the face of the Covidian onslaught of institutionalized lies and Soviet-grade censorship, one doesn't know whether to laugh or cry.

And when we consider that virtually all those he endorses as exemplars of propaganda-savvy journalism—people such as Chris Hedges, Patrick Lawrence, Jonathan Cook, Diana Johnstone, Caitlin Johnstone all of whose work I have frequently and enthusiastically championed over the years—took the same cud-chewing path, the sense of farce only grows.

The same can be said of many of the outlets (*The Grayzone, MintPress News, Media Lens, Declassified UK, Alborada, The Electronic Intifada, WSWS, ZNet, ICH, CounterPunch, Independent Australia, Globetrotter*) he suggests as being particularly wise to the wiles of elite-sponsored influence operations.

Who, the question thus occurs to me, is actually living in a "a deep bath of righteousness" that impedes the ability to access the truths that lie beyond the "official version" of our past and present?

Who exactly is failing to respond to the presence of fascistic tendencies in our midst?

If I didn't know better, I'd swear it was John and his merry band of crack propaganda dissectors.

Is it that hard for them to see the shadow of fascism in the now heavily documented collaboration between the US government and Big Tech in censoring opinions that go counter to the government's and Big Pharma's desired discourse on Covid?

Is it really difficult for them to see the presence of the same dark forces in the US government's insouciant abrogation of the Nuremberg principle relating to informed consent and medical experimentation?

Are they not troubled by the fact that the experimental vaccines that were sold to the population on the basis of their ability to stop infection do not do that? Or that this was known to anyone who read the FDA briefing papers published when these injections were unleashed on the public?

Does this count as a major "propaganda problem" worth looking into?

Do they care about the millions of people who lost their jobs over these lies, and of course the government's abject disdain for the longstanding statutory right to object to medical treatment on religious grounds?

As long-time mavens of foreign policy, have they looked into the mafia-like nature of the vaccine contracts forced upon sovereign countries around the world?

Being the great sleuths of information-hiding that they are, did it raise any suspicions in them when Pfizer sought to keep all clinical information relating to the vaccine trials under wraps for 75 years?

And being the good progressives they are, did the enormous upward transfer of wealth that took place during the years of the Covid state of exception trouble them?

Did it light any suspicions that all this hullabaloo might not just be about health?

Have they organized support groups and action plans for the billions of children around the world whose lives were thrown into chaos by the useless quarantine and masking that was foisted upon them, and who, in all likelihood will never recover the years of developmental progress lost to this program of senseless cruelty?

I could go on.

As far as I can tell, the answer to all these questions is a resounding "NO!"

I am truly grateful for all that John Pilger and his companions in the leftist propaganda dissection cadres have taught me over the years. But as Ortega y Gasset said, a public intellectual is only as good as his ability to remain at the "height of his times."

Sadly, this group of otherwise talented individuals has failed this test, badly, over the last two-plus years.

Why these self-proclaimed uncoverers of camouflaged realities suddenly decided to unsee what was happening before their eyes is a job for future historians.

But if I had to hazard a guess today, I'd say that it had a lot to do with all the usual human things like fear of losing friends and prestige, or being seen by ideological enforcers on their side as going over to the enemy. All of which is fine and understandable.

But if that is the case, is it too much to publicly admit now that you missed the boat on this important story?

And if you can't manage that, could you, for your own sake if nothing else, at least stop issuing sermons on topics like "how propaganda works" for the foreseeable future?

19 September 2022

SPEED BUMPS

The state of Oaxaca, in the south of Mexico, is an extraordinarily beautiful place with gorgeous beaches and an interior defined by both barren and densely forested mountains. But more impressive still is the human diversity of the place. Unlike many other areas of the vast Mexican state, the region's indigenous cultures continue to live in a relatively high state of cohesion and dignity.

There is one thing, however, that is absolutely horrendous there: driving. And not for the reasons you at first might think.

Yes, some of the interior roads are in ill repair. But what makes driving hell in Oaxaca are the speed bumps, which are of a huge, consistently chassis-scraping size, and are deployed at very tight intervals along most every road or highway. And this is, in my experience, in contrast to what I've seen in other parts of Mexico.

Upon returning home after my first visit to Oaxaca I couldn't get those speed bumps out of my mind. And once on the subject, I couldn't help noticing how many of them had sprung up in very recent years in Connecticut, especially in the impoverished city of Hartford where I live.

And it got me thinking about what, if anything, the deployment of these cultural artifacts in Oaxaca, and increasingly in places like Hartford might indicate about the broader cultural reality within which they are embedded.

The idea of public space that developed in the late medieval and early modern periods was anchored, above all, in a revolution of the idea of interpersonal trust. This was in sharp contrast to the life of the manor from whence many of these first free dwellers of the *bourgs* (as in the root word of bourgeoisie) had come, where "might" literally did make "right," and fear rather than trust was the dominant social currency.

Though scholars from northern Europe have often suggested

otherwise, Spain was rather well advanced on the road to urbanization when settlers from the Iberian Peninsula began their conquest and pillage of the Americas, as can be seen in the splendid and formulaic sturdiness of walled cities like Havana, San Juan and Cartagena, Colombia.

But for a number of geographical, political and cultural reasons the Spanish attempt to "civilize"—derived from the same Latin root that gave us the terms "city" and citizens—Oaxaca fell well short of their results in other places. Aware that conquest as they fully desired it was probably unachievable there, the Spaniards eventually switched from a strategy of total domination to one of containment. If the native Zapotecs and Mixtecs could not be routed, they would at least have to be controlled.

According to anthropologist Laura Nader, this standoff generated a fascinating dialogue of "controlling cultural practices" between the Spanish elites (and subsequently those of the Mexican state) and the authorities of indigenous communities over the ensuing decades and centuries.

What the external and internal imposers of these controlling practices had in common was a deep distrust in the idea that ordinary people, if left to their own devices, were capable of safeguarding what they considered core civic values. And of course when individuals are told repeatedly that they can't be trusted to exercise civic responsibility, they tend to live down to the expectations, something which, of course, reifies the elite belief in the need to impose ever more stringent controlling practices.

It could be argued, and I think I'd largely agree, that as the weaker party of a cultural clash with a force known for its skill at dismantling other cultures, the top-down approach of the indigenous authorities is mostly justified, and that it is a key reason why the native cultures in Oaxaca are as relatively intact as they are.

But it still does not obviate the fact that individuals there are in many ways seen by those in charge in Mexico City and in their local governments as needing constant and quite palpable tutelage in the conduct of their civic lives.

Hence the existence of those muffler-massacring and spine-crushing speed bumps everywhere you go.

For all of its obvious failures, the US was for a long time distinguished from Mexico and from many other societies around the world by its leaders' belief that if left to their own devices within a broad set of legal and ethical guidelines, citizens will more often than not find successful ways of addressing and resolving the collective's more pressing existential concerns.

This, I suspect, is why I had little or no engagement with speed bumps during my first four or so decades as a licensed driver.

But that's all gone now.

In the new US, I am, like most of my fellow citizens, considered by those in power to be inherently unable to recognize what is good for myself, or the overall good of the community in which I live. Hence their supposed need to constantly nudge me and most others toward "correct" personal and social decisions.

And speed bumps, which presume my inherent recklessness and irresponsibility as a driver and citizen are, of course, but one of the many infantilizing "controlling practices" with which we are now assaulted daily.

Are you prepared for the snowstorm? The hurricane? Are you wearing your mask correctly? Did you recycle your disposables? Buckle your seatbelt? Make sure your child is wearing a bike helmet? Have you done an analysis of your state of erectile health? Did you use the right pronouns? Did you assume the core fragility and lack of resilience of your interlocutor(s) before openly affirming how you see or interpret this or that aspect of reality?

None of this is to say that the actions suggested above are inherently problematic or bad, but to say that the practice of constantly instructing us about matters that free citizens have long known how to respond to in sensible ways, is in no way accidental or innocent. It is, rather, part of a clear campaign to render us all impervious to the natural development and deployment of our own social instincts.

And to deprive people of the ability to address day-to-day challenges independently through the development of their own personal sensibilities is to effectively keep them in a childish state of dependence before those who the media holds up as "experts" and "authorities." This, as if history is not littered with the enormous damage done by the abject idiocy of such people. As if getting a certain degree or title shields one from the corrosive presence of vanity, greed and self-deception when making judgments.

But this is precisely what we have been told *ad nauseam* over the last 30 months.

And because so many people have been deprived of the sense of real security that only a combination of hands-on love and personal introspection can bring, millions have passively gone along with this preposterous premise.

Human beings live by stories. The powerful, knowing this, work overtime to furnish them for us, with the proviso, of course, that the narratives exalt "their" values and denigrate those they see as having the potential to make others question their wisdom and omnipotence.

And they know, moreover, that we are creatures of habit and that by placing seemingly innocent but in fact ideologically charged objects like speed bumps in our midst, or establishing ritual practices imbued with clear, if at the same time subtle, ideological messages, they can often bring us around to their way of interpreting reality.

We, however, have enormous storytelling and ritual-making capacities of our own. But they can only be accessed and developed if we give ourselves the time and the silence needed to reflect on what it is we really know, feel and desire, not in the context of the pre-masticated options provided by supposedly wise and authoritative others, but in the wonderful silence of our own private imagination, and our own singular way of perceiving and relating to the unending and mind-boggling mystery of life.

This done, we must, as the deeply social and yarn-spinning creatures we are, then share our views as fearlessly as we can with others in the hope that people at both ends of the dialogue might infect still others with the hope-spawning idea that we were put on this earth to be a good deal more than passive receptacles of the self-serving verbal and symbolic discourses of our alleged masters.

Think that a speed bump is just a speed bump?

Think again.

Think it's an accident that so many practices that had no proven epidemiological effectiveness—like masks, social distancing, plexiglass barriers, and draconian regimes of social separation—all also just happened to be excellent ways of inhibiting "unofficial" storytelling, and the sense of solidarity and individual empowerment it always brings?

Think again.

These are classic "controlling practices" designed to gradually leach from each and every one of us—and most infuriatingly those not yet fully socialized—what is arguably our greatest instinctual drive: the desire to weave stories of our own in the company of others that remind us not of what they tell us we are and must be for them, but of the sense of dignity that we all want to feel and, to the best of our abilities, extend to others.

It's time we made more time for the construction and maintenance of these laboratories of spiritual freedom.

3 October 2022

DOCTORS WHO LIVE IN FEAR AND PROMOTE IT IN OTHERS

Fear is a ubiquitous and essential part of the human experience. Indeed, a good case could be made that it is the driving force in the lives of many, if not most human beings. It is the terror of knowing our lives are finite and likely to be marked, especially toward their ends, by considerable pain and tragedy that has given rise to most religions, and from there—though today's legions of secular presentists might be loathe to admit it—much of what we generally refer to as artistic culture.

To admit the ubiquity and power of fear, however, is not to say that we are condemned to live perpetually in its thrall. In fact, the very ideas of human dignity and human progress depend precisely on our ability to, in some way, train ourselves to repel or overlook its enormous paralyzing powers.

Prudent cultural leaders know this. And it is why, since the beginning of human civilization, they have assiduously sought to identify and celebrate the members of their collectives who are, or appear to be, most impervious to fright. They do so not only as a way of symbolically expressing the group's thanks for the execution of difficult and perilous tasks, but also to promote the development of courage—derived from the Latin word for heart—among the young.

For much of history, most of these heroes were celebrated for their ability to overcome fear and act courageously in the face of physical annihilation on the battlefield.

But in most societies there has also always been a smaller subset of people venerated for their ability to heal, which is to say, to labor calmly and compassionately day after day in the presence of heartbreaking human diminishment and impending death.

To be reminded of the fragility of life and the omnipresence of death each day is not easy, as it necessarily forces the healer to fixate upon the reality of their own mortality. We have traditionally honored these people precisely for their ability—honed through mental and spiritual discipline—to face daily life in this liminal netherworld with equanimity.

I am the son, grandson, brother, nephew (x3) and first cousin (x3) of doctors. I have heard stories of doctor-patient relationships my whole life. At first, I assimilated them as one might assimilate entertaining tales on TV.

But as I grew older and began to address the issues of anxiety and fear in my own life, I came to think about them in a very different way. A crystalizing moment came when talking with my father about the Polio epidemic of 1952, and how as an intern he had been assigned work on the Polio ward of Boston City Hospital at the height of the plague.

"Weren't you frightened?" I asked him. He said, "Of course I was. But it was my job as a physician-in-training to overcome my fear so I could stay calm and serve my patients."

My father was a highly sensitive and deeply emotional man, not exactly your classic low-pulse, affectively distant sort of person.

But the imperative of calming the self or to be in a position to reassure and heal others never left him. How do I know? From the hundreds of spontaneous demonstrations sincere, and at times, tearful, second-hand appreciations I have received throughout the years from his patients and their immediate families.

Given his essential nature, I can only imagine the titanic effort it took for him to develop and maintain this compassionate courage in the course of his career.

Lately, however, it seems we have witnessed a strange and ominous inversion of this long-standing model of physician comportment.

I noticed the first signs during my time as an undergrad at a college known for a superb pre-med program. Talking with my friends in the program about their goals, I was struck by the near total lack—if even in a posing and insincere way—of interest in the healing vocation my father and uncles had led me to believe doctoring was all about. There was, however, no shortage of talk about money, big houses and golf club memberships.

Well, those contemporaries of mine are now at the most senior levels of medical leadership in this country. And the last two and a half years have shown us exactly what happens when we allow one of the most important, dare I say sacred, social vocations to be taken over by a cadre of comfort-seeking arrivistes.

Under the loving tutelage of Big Pharma and the pernicious belief, spread by our medical institutions, that healing is largely, if not exclusively, a technical and procedural matter, they have been allowed, if not encouraged to ignore the always enormous spiritual component of the process. A process which, of course, begins with their own personal struggle against existential angst.

"Why go there, if you don't have to?" they might ask.

Answer: You go there, as every doctor once used to know, so that you can transcend your own natural smallness and enter into the realm of empathy and compassion for the patient.

You go there so you will understand as clear as the day is light and the night is dark, that no dying person should ever be left alone, never mind under the pretext of a "deadly" respiratory disease that leaves 99.85 percent of its victims alive.

You go there so that you will understand in the same way you know your own child is beautiful that medication should never be forced upon an individual in the name of the greater good—never mind one engineered by a voracious and immoral corporate entity—and that to do so is a grave insult to human dignity.

You go there so that you will understand that denying help to a suffering person for any reason, never mind so that Big Pharma can up the panic level to enhance vaccine sales, is a crime.

You go there, so that when you are threatened with demotion or firing by heartless bureaucrats aligned with the Pharma criminals, you will have an independent moral framework—transcendent of the game of professional punishments and rewards—to make sense of your circumstance, and to guide you in the process of reconstructing your life on a more meaningful and enduring basis.

You go there is, in short, to not become, like so many of your colleagues, a kiss-up, kick-down, fear-promoting cypher who brings daily discredit to one of the world's oldest and most noble vocations.

18 October 2022

STRAIGHT LINES, CIRCLES AND THE
ART OF STAYING HUMAN

Many, if not most, who question the approach that has been taken to controlling Covid are mystified, when they are not frankly enraged, by how so many people they took to be thoughtful and intelligent have failed to engage in any meaningful way with the available empirical evidence on the public health measures proposed and enacted by our public institutions. Similarly vexing and infuriating to many of us has been the failure of these people to even begin to acknowledge the copious damage generated by these same measures.

Many theses have been advanced to explain this sudden and massive outbreak of know-nothingism across the so-called developed world.

Several of them have centered the ability of hugely powerful corporate interests, working hand-in-glove with captured governments, to censor and intimidate would-be thought leaders into silence. This is obviously a huge factor. But, in my view, it only gets us so far.

Why?

Because this self-evident plague of silence and critical listlessness has been accompanied at every step by a consciously produced blizzard of nonsense emanating from the same precincts of alleged intellectual refinement, its most oft-repeated and ridiculous element being the notion that science is a fixed canon of laws as opposed to an open and ever-evolving process of trial and error.

That so many working scientists and other highly credentialed people signed on, actively or passively, to this primitive and infantile premise during the preceding 30 months constitutes a severe indictment of our educational establishment.

It shows that most of the people paid by society to think do not reflect in any regular or systematic way upon the epistemologies, or frameworks of meaning, within which they operate.

And if, as it appears, these people know or care little about founding premises of their own fields of inquiry, it is a good bet that they've seldom if ever pondered the still broader, and historically specific cultural assumptions from which many of these same disciplinary practices sprang.

Like?

Like, for example, our culturally-generated understanding of time.

Most of us think about time a lot. But how many of us think about *how* we think about time?

Indeed, if you asked most people—including myself until I was forced to engage with the late 19th and early 20th-century clash between centralizing and peripheral nationalisms in Spain—about this you would be met with blank stares. Most assume, as I once did, that time just *is*, and that it proceeds inexorably and in a linear fashion into the future, and away from the past.

What I was forced to confront back then, however, was that this was a relatively new way of understanding the passage of time, one inextricably linked to the rise of modernity in Europe toward the end of the 15th century, and with it—among many other things—the advent of the nation-state and the idea of inexorable human progress through scientific discovery.

Before this, many if not most cultures viewed time in cyclical terms, meaning that they created and lived by a concept of time that provided a built-in mental and spiritual allowance for, and explanation of, humanity's tendency to err, regress, and engage from time to time in the angry and irrational destruction of the greatest fruits of its collective labors.

Or to put it in theological terms, they lived a concept of time that made room for the idea of what most Christian traditions call original sin.

Linear time, in contrast, generally leaves man alone with his own permanent visions of perfectibility. Heady stuff. And no doubt an enormous factor in the general improvement of our material circumstance over these last five or so centuries. To believe you are in control is, at least in some unquantifiable way, to be more in control and capable of making positive things happen in your immediate environs.

But what happens, as is inevitable, when the palpable fruits of a particular way of being and thinking diminish as the particular historical zeitgeist it inspired runs out of energy?

Well, if your concept of time is cyclical you can much more easily allow yourself to admit what is going on, and to begin to make adjustments that will allow for a more fruitful engagement with the changing reality.

If, however, the only concept of time you've ever known is linear, you're in a pretty bad spot. Under this paradigm of time, there is, in effect, no turning back. Rather, there is a tendency to engage in a compulsive doubling and tripling down on the techniques that at least a part of you knows are not working as well as they once did, and a consequent need to forcefully block out anyone and anything that might further feed that doubting part of your being.

The results of this frantic and self-defeating mindset are there for all who want to see them in our culture.

We see this lack of "cyclical consciousness" in the inability of so many people to engage with the issues of human diminishment and death with a minimal level of equanimity, grace and proportion, something that in my view goes a long way toward explaining the extremely hysterical reaction of so many of our fellow citizens to the spread of the SARS-CoV-2 virus.

We see it in the pitiful (that is, if it weren't so unbelievably dangerous) mindset of our foreign policy elites. As purblind acolytes of the school of linear time, they literally cannot imagine a world in which the US "right" to command, direct and sack the treasures of other peoples of the world does not exist. Thus, despite the country's self-evident loss of vital energy and wealth, they cannot even begin to conceive of executing a wise and artful curl off of what they still insist on seeing as the endless, railroad-straight path to ever-greater levels of American supremacy.

And now we are observing it most acutely in our culture's approach to the theory and practice of science in general, and medicine in particular.

Modernity's most important conceptual innovation, as I suggested above, was granting mankind permission to see the non-human elements of the world as amenable not just to the intentions of God, but also to our own quite earthly designs and desires.

That this effective declaration of war on nature produced enormous material benefits for at least some of the world's inhabitants, there can be no denying. And those that, following the latest fad, flippantly suggest this was not so, only demonstrate their cultural ignorance.

However, to defend the accomplishments of modernity and its beloved offspring, empirically-driven science, is not necessarily to say that this linear, man vs. nature model of thinking can or will produce ever-increasing, or even constant levels of benefit over time.

Like people, paradigms get tired, mostly because the humans that work within them increasingly lose touch with the problems that originally elicited in them the intense and sacrifice-laden drive to create urgently desired new things.

But humans aren't always very good at recognizing when they have begun going through the motions. This is especially so with those in the thrall of a purely linear vision of time in which the perennial reality of intellectual and spiritual regression is afforded no legitimate space.

The results are what we might call zombie institutions, places with all—and often much more—of the imposing physical manifestations of their past glory, but very little of the urgent, human and existentially-driven creativity that made them necessary and effective.

And there is a surefire way of knowing when social institutions have entered this phase of their existence, one known to all who have studied the decline of Spain—the world's first modern empire—and the concurrent rise of Baroque culture within it.

It is the ever-widening gap between the actual accomplishments of key social institutions and the degree of verbal and symbolic self-aggrandizement generated on their behalf.

When American medicine was actually producing miracle cures and extending the lifespan of the citizenry, its actions spoke for themselves. Little PR was necessary. However, now—as most studies on US life expectancy indicate—that burst of creativity has come to its end and has been replaced by arcane schemes designed not to cure, but to extend the medical industry's profitability and level of control over citizen lives, we are being ceaselessly commanded to salute our noble doctors and the heartless Pharma corporations that control their practices.

And we have discovered, sadly, that few of those working within this baroque hall of mirrors have the critical acuity or moral courage to admit what they and the institutions within which they work have actually become.

And even sadder still is the tendency of those who don't work within the medical industrial complex, but share its educational sociology, to continue to nostalgically insist out of an apparent fear of betraying their caste and its rigidly linear creed of human progress, that there is a direct line of moral and scientific continuity between say the first great doctor-hygienists, whose work probably saved millions, and an Anthony Fauci, who produced an unneeded and ineffective pandemic response that ruined life for millions.

So, to return to our initial question, "Why do so many refuse to see what is right before their eyes?"

Because doing so would require them to adopt an entirely new cosmovision, one in which linear progress is not a metaphysical guarantee, but a noble aspiration in a road of life that, as the pre-moderns knew all too well, always has more rocky turns than expanses of straight and well-paved highway.

2 November 2022

THE SCHOOL OF FRIENDSHIP

Two Saturdays ago, I had a magical experience. I returned to my late mother's hometown for a memorial service for one of her best friends—one of three she had known from the time she was five—and exchanged stories at graveside and then at a nearby restaurant with the two survivors about the group's eight decades of unbroken and always warm friendships.

Coming to know one's parents is a lifelong pursuit. As we age we are forever mixing and remixing our memories of them in the hope of composing a more or less finished portrait of who they were for us, and the world at large.

Doing so is not, at least for me, an occasional excursion into nostalgia. Rather, it is a constant pursuit, fueled by a perhaps vain desire to continually grow in consciousness as I traipse toward my own final, fateful day. And this is so for a simple reason. I will forever be the son of my parents, and who they were, or were not, is deeply embedded in me.

That our memories are unreliable is, of course, well-known. But is also well-known that, lest a person dissolve into a hapless sack of fleeting and fragmentary sensations (something that seems to be the goal of many educators and promoters of popular culture today), we must take on the task of building a functional identity from the many shards of memory we carry inside.

Is there a method for this? I'm not sure.

But I believe there are certain habits that can help, like keeping a careful inventory of the memories—or for me as an intensely auditory and visual person, the pleasing "voice recordings" and "place pictures"—to which we return again and again in the course of our lives. In reliving these moments of spiritual warmth and fullness we not only find solace in times of difficulty, but remind ourselves, in the midst of the faux cornucopia of consumer culture, of what our inner selves truly desire as we move through time.

"Listening" to myself in this way, I have been surprised in recent years by how my childhood memories of my mother's hometown, where I only spent weekends and two-week summer stretches with my grandparents, uncle and aunt have come to eclipse those of the place where I grew up day-to-day, happily went to school and played hockey, had my first loves, and gulped those first illicit beers with the buds.

Odd no?

Well, the other day I think I stumbled onto an explanation. My mother's Leominster, the declining mill town 20 minutes from my own, was a place where everyone was someone and where, when I walked down Main Street hand-in-hand with my grandfather, or went to early Mass and picked up the newspaper with my uncle, there was always time for a story to be exchanged. I thus received constant reminders that every ostensibly mundane and practical encounter with others is an opportunity to try and understand a bit more about them and their world.

But even more important than this was the way my mother's family looked at friendship. It started with the premise that just about everyone with whom you habitually crossed paths was worthy of it, and that, short of outright acts of lying or hostility, that bond would continue, in one form of another, in perpetuity.

Needless to say, this outlook placed a premium on tolerance. When, during the Saturday afternoon cocktail parties my grandmother and grandfather—a 25-year member of the school committee and local Democratic party leader—would throw, Jimmy Foster would show up, as they used to say, "half-cocked" or Doc McHugh would get a little carried away with his own brilliance, it was, like so many other similar things that occurred, just another colorful part of life

And therein lies, a wonderful and perhaps revealing paradox. Those Leominster Smiths were the furthest thing in the world from moral relativists. They had deep, deep convictions rooted in both their Catholic faith and what might be termed an Irish post-colonial hatred of lying, phoniness, bullying and injustice. And if you crossed one of those lines, you would hear about it, up front, in a hurry.

But until "that time," you were a trusted friend with all your quirks, foibles and sometimes petty concerns.

For my mother, as with my uncle and aunt, this mixture of deep conviction and profound tolerance gifted them with extraordinarily long friendships with very diverse types of people.

When my very conservative uncle died, his high-powered friend of 70 years, and former member of Nixon's enemies list, showed up from Washington to deliver a eulogy.

During the last decades of her life the best friends of my aunt, whose Catholicism could perhaps best be described as Tridentine, was a gay couple.

And as for my mother, whose diverse four-girl posse included a hard-driving, divorced businesswoman who had spent long years in Australia, a four-time cancer survivor, wife, mother and entrepreneur, and a gracious and athletic beauty happily married to the same man for 70 years, "that time" to end or even question the fundamentals of their friendship, of course, never came. And so it was in most every one of the many other warm friendships she cultivated and enjoyed in her life.

And two Saturdays back, my sister and I reveled not only in the stories lived and told during the preceding eight decades, but also the certain knowledge we had attended, through my mother and her family's extraordinary gift for creating and maintaining friendships, a school much more important than the ones from which we had received our fancy degrees.

Could it be, in these times of division and pressure to quickly enlist with one side or another of a given social or ideological position, those Leominster Smiths were on to something important?

Might it be that what passes today for ideological convictions, in our supposedly terminally divided country, are nothing of the sort, but rather labels to which many quickly and lightly affix themselves precisely because they haven't really thought deeply about what they believe and why, but don't want to be seen as being out of step, or of not having really done their homework?

Perhaps it is time to remind them what my mother's family knew and taught by example: that every person is an opportunity for learning and that real people of conviction don't fear opposing opinions, or have the slightest need to silence or censor those with whom they appear to disagree.

5 November 2022

AFTERWORD

n times of pain we emit groans and cries. We do so most obviously to elicit help. But as a wise music therapist friend and student of Negro spirituals reminded me, we also do so to release the embedded knots of pain and trauma from our bodies. In other words, to express deep feelings of hurt and dismay in the absence of listeners is never in vain as it lessens your burden and makes it easier to fight another day.

When the Covid cloud descended upon us, I began to groan and cry through my essays, as writers tend to do. And being a student of history, I did so with little hope of being heard or responded to.

Then, a funny thing happened. Someone out there sent back a message, someone who saw in my verbal shouts and those of others the kernel of something new and powerful, the possibility of building a community that would reignite the once powerful but now flickering flames of human dignity, intellectual integrity and individual freedom.

That person was Jeffrey Tucker and the dynamic ideologically diverse community he founded in the service of these goals is Brownstone Institute.

If we ever emerge from the morass we are in, I am convinced that future historians will see Brownstone for what it is, and has been during the short time since its founding: a bulwark of the insurgency against those who in their mechanistic hubris would have renounce so much of what we know makes us human.

I am proud to be part of that community and hope that in some small way this book contributes to its strength and future growth, and perhaps even to the strength and growth of the larger movement to recover our stolen freedoms

INDEX

www.ingramcontent.com/pod-product-compliance
Lightning Source LLC
Chambersburg PA
CBHW030914090426
4737CB0000078/195